Don't Collude with Your E… Navigating the Landscape of Feelings for a B… 130+ Strategies

DCWYE. Don't Collude with Your Emotions: Navigating the Landscape of Feelings for a Balanced Life, 130+ Strategies

By Jo Tagliarini, BACP BA

This interactive journal is crafted to aid young children, young adults, and even your inner child in cultivating practical tools and clever techniques to to master their emotions in healthy and positive ways.

The strategies and insights conveyed in this journal are gleaned from the author's extensive experience in counseling and study of neuropsychology. *Nevertheless, this book does not act as a substitute for professional advice or treatment from a licensed psychologist, therapist, or counselor.*

The author strongly urges all readers to seek professional guidance if they grapple with emotional regulation or confront mental health challenges. Every person possesses unique traits and may necessitate customized guidance and support on their distinct emotional journey. This journal is designed to complement their resources, allowing sojourners to delve further into the realm of self-regulation and explore additional techniques.

By engaging with this journal, readers can refine their self-regulation skills and cultivate a profound understanding of how to navigate their emotions when confronted with adversities. The author aspires for this journal to be an invaluable resource not only for parents, teachers, and counselors who interact with children but also for the reader themselves.

Kindly note that this journal does not replace personalized therapeutic interventions, as individual needs and circumstances may differ. The author encourages a collaborative approach, combining the guidance offered within this book with professional support, to ensure optimal emotional well-being and growth for each and every reader.

The Power of Action over Emotion

In this journal, "DCWYE" we explore a vital concept: acknowledging emotions without letting them control us.

As a counselor, I understand the prevailing idea that we should listen to our feelings and let them guide us. It seems intuitive, even spiritual. However, there's a catch. Our emotions are heavily influenced by our past experiences; they're vessels of memories. Consequently, when we allow our feelings to dictate our actions, we're essentially traveling back in time, repeatedly getting stuck in our personal histories.

While our brain's alarm bells might ring when we perceive something as unsafe, it doesn't always mean we're in physical danger. Yet, to our brains, it feels just like that. So, we make excuses, invite fear or anxiety for tea and biscuits, and soon find ourselves frozen in time.

If we perpetually let our feelings guide our decisions, we'll never expand our horizons or break free from our comfort zones. We'll remain ensnared by our pasts. But if feelings shouldn't be our compass, then what should?

Our actions!

To make a profound shift, our actions must lead the way, even when we don't "feel" like it. I'm no exception; there are days I don't "feel" like going to the gym, eating healthily, or giving compliments to colleagues. However, because I've turned these into habits, I don't consider my feelings when deciding. I simply go to the gym, eat healthily, and offer compliments. And afterward, I'm always happier for it.

Here's a breakdown of DCWYE:

Acknowledge Your Emotions: Emotions are an integral part of being human. They provide insights into how we perceive and react to situations. So, acknowledging them is crucial.

Avoid Dwelling on Negative Emotions: The phrase "don't collude with your emotions" advises against dwelling excessively on unhelpful or negative emotions. We can sometimes get caught in cycles of rumination, which only worsen our emotional state.

Emotional Regulation: DCWYE encourages emotional regulation, meaning managing emotions in healthy ways. This includes:

- Recognizing and Labeling Emotions: Identifying and labeling emotions can help us understand what we're feeling.
- Acceptance: Embracing our emotions, both positive and negative, without judgment.
- Healthy Expression: Finding productive outlets for our emotions, such as talking, writing, art, or physical activities.
- Problem Solving: Using our emotions as motivation to find solutions or make positive life changes.
- Prevent Overwhelming Emotions: Especially negative ones like anger, anxiety, or sadness. DCWYE advises against letting these emotions take the reins of your life.

In essence, this journal promotes emotional self-awareness and regulation, ensuring that emotions are our allies rather than our captors.

Welcome to "DCWYE" a journey of self-discovery and emotional growth. As you open the pages of this journal, you'll find a world where emotions become vibrant characters on a grand stage, each contributing to the intricate tapestry of your life.

You have the freedom to dive into this journal wherever your heart desires – whether following a systematic approach or leaping right in. As you engage with each strategy, mark the boxes to track your progress, but remember, there's no need to rush. Take pleasure in each moment, and feel free to use this resource daily, weekly, or with breaks in between.

Upon completion, take time to digest and meditate on the wisdom within. Consider sharing your discoveries with a trusted friend, family member, or counselor, as you embark on this enchanting journey of self-discovery.

Within these pages, you'll find <u>Over 130 Ingenious Strategies</u> interwoven into a metaphorical and allegorical narrative. As you delve into the world of emotional intelligence, be guided by a sense of whimsy and wonder. Prepare some colors and keep a dictionary handy if needed, as you engage with the artistic expressions within.

This unique and expressive journal serves as a gateway to imagination, visualization, and the art of crafting and reshaping thought habits that may be holding you back. It offers a mosaic of insights, imparting the wisdom that emotions, much like actors in a play, don't control the entire storyline of your life. Feeling like a failure, for example, is just one role they assume, not the entire script itself.

Embrace the enchantment of understanding emotions as fleeting actors in the grand theater of life. Immerse yourself in metaphorical landscapes where fostering new habits and breaking free from the hold of emotional patterns resembles tending a garden or guiding a ship through turbulent seas. This allegorical adventure wonderfully reflects the journey of recognizing, embracing, and reshaping feelings into tools of empowerment.

– now,
where would you like to embark on this transformative journey?

☑

IMAGINE THIS:

Within the nooks and crannies of this brainy canvas, pour in splendid words about you. Let the splendidness of joy, hope, and success cascade like liquid gold, filling up your thoughts with a shimmering glow.

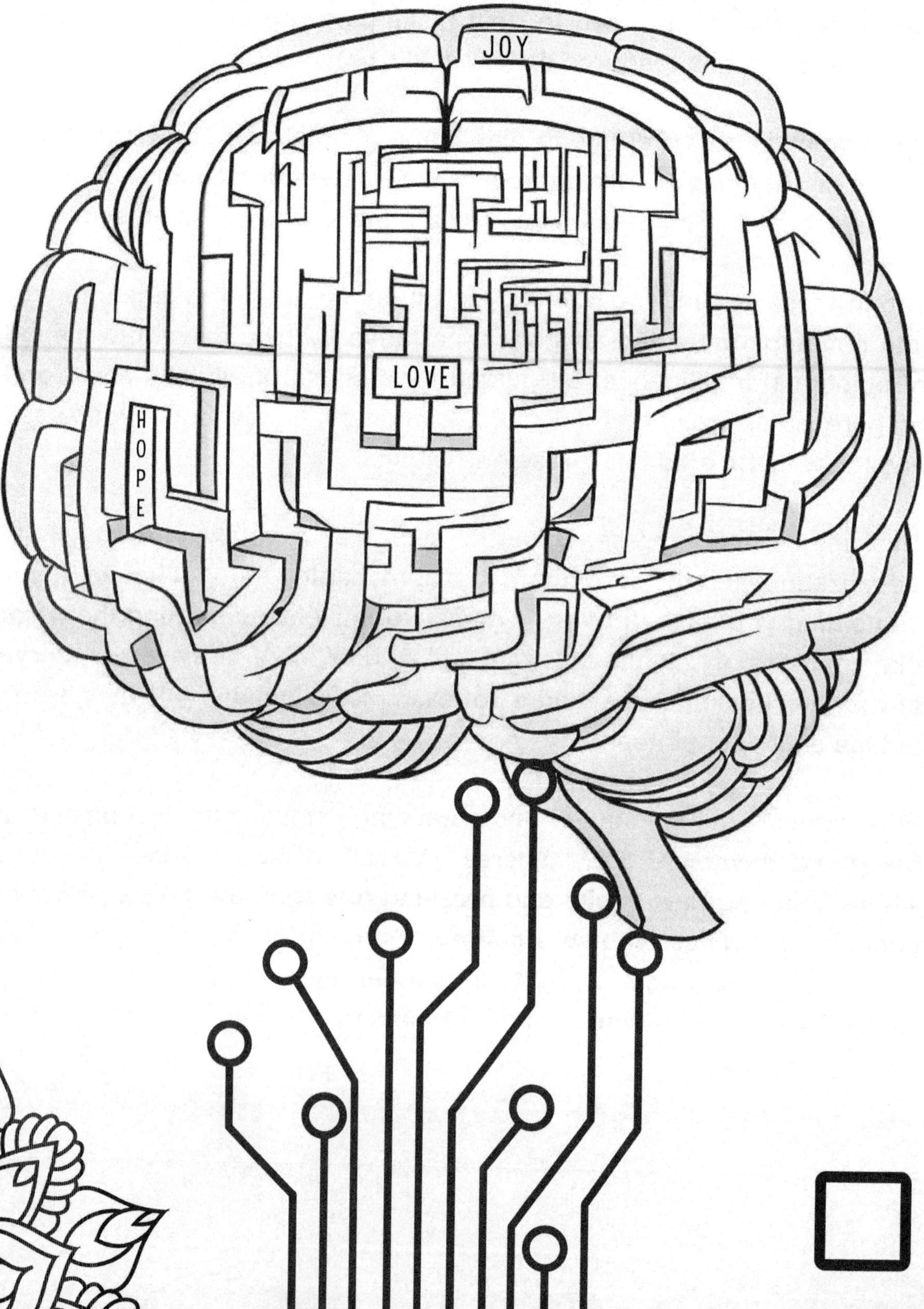

PICTURE THIS:

Those very words you penned on the previous sheet, let them cascade down like a gentle stream into the chambers of your heart. How does it feel, my friend, to witness those words meandering and trickling, turning your heart into a reservoir of wonder?

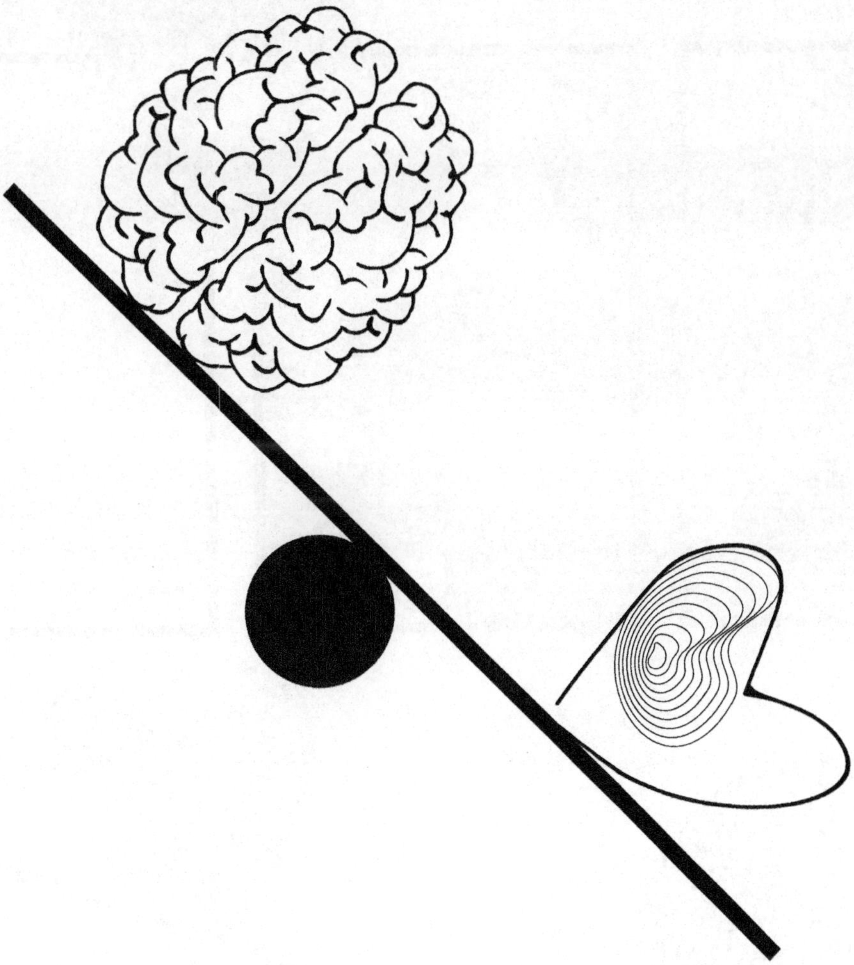

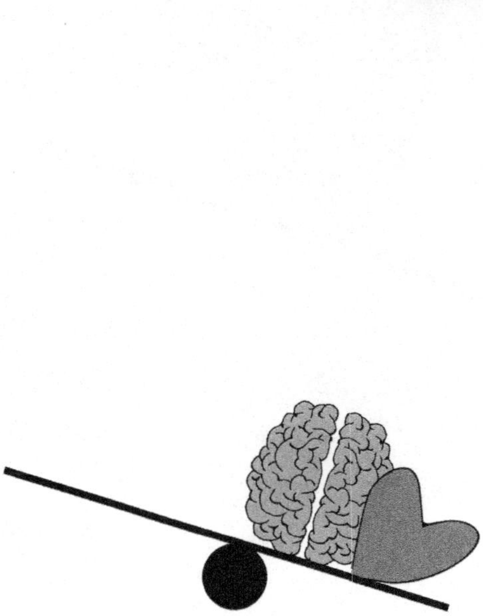

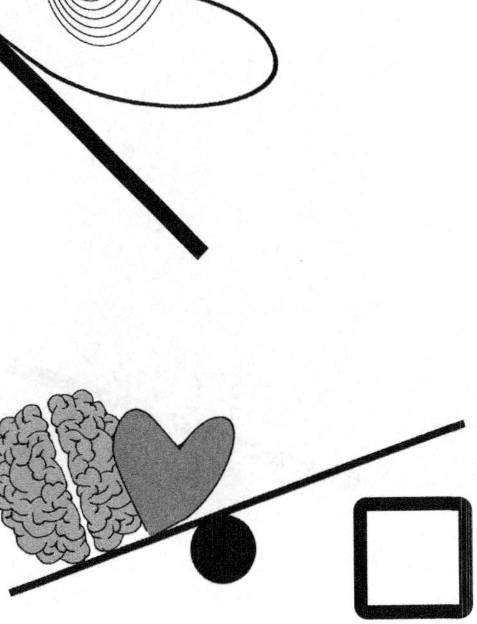

F.E.A.R CATALYST:

(False Expectations Appearing Real)

Turning fear into an excuse is a common trap. Instead, use fear as a catalyst for growth by setting achievable goals and taking small steps forward. This strategy helps you confront fear while steadily progressing toward your objectives.

DIALOGUES WITH YOUR HEART:

Speak with your emotions, like wise old explorers sharing tales around a campfire.

- "Sitting with my emotions felt like chatting with ancient mariners about their ocean journeys."

FROM CHAOS TO CLARITY:
SCRIBBLES OF HOPE:

Imagine unraveling the thoughts, letting lines and scribbles find their place within the squares where glimmers of truth, hope, and words of joy reside.

SHINE A LIGHT ON THEM:

Expose emotions to the sun like a hidden treasure map, so their power diminishes.

- "Just as a spyglass unveils secrets, revealing emotions lessens their grip."

GROUNDED IN THE MOMENT:

To remain grounded in the moment, jot down five things you can see, four things you can hear, three things you can smell, two things you can taste, and one thing you can feel with your hands around you.

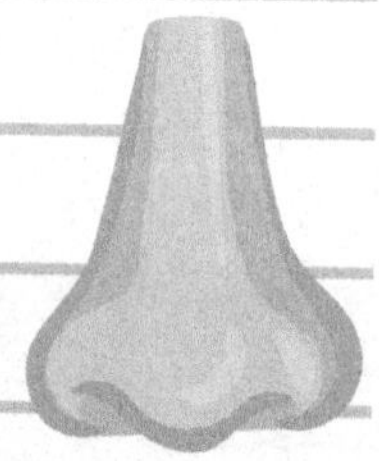

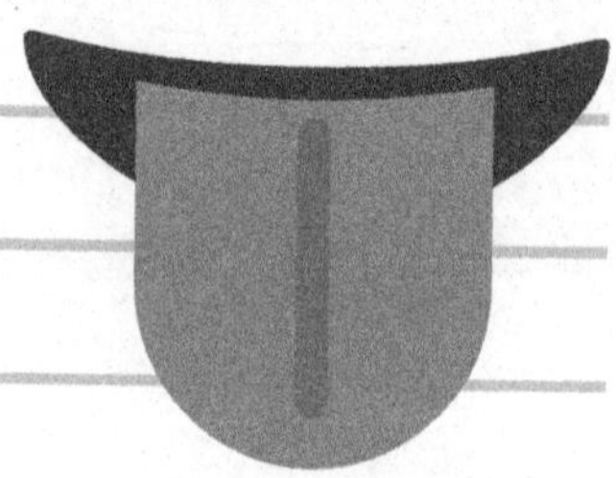

Fill these talking boxes with any worries. then below. let the very same boxes brim with the truths and hopes that cast away anxiety.

DUAL-HAND DA VINCI DOODLES:

Start by letting both your hands dance across the page, creating lines that intertwine like mischievous partners in a playful game. Imagine your lines forming whimsical squiggles, as if they're revealing secrets from a magical garden. This imaginative activity not only brings joy but also sharpens your hands' fine motor skills, making them more skillful as they weave basic lines into marvelous scenes. It's a bit like Michelangelo's idea of sculpting to unveil an angel from stone. Just as he found hidden beauty, you'll discover wonder in your doodles, sweeping away any shadowy thoughts that try to linger.

DUAL-HAND DA VINCI DOODLES

NOW-NATURE OBSERVER:

Tune into the now. watch thoughts flutter by like curious creatures in a secret garden. Let your mind be the gentle breeze that rustles their wings.

MUSCLE MEMORY:

Imagine you're a puppet master of your own body. Flex and release your muscles, guiding tension away like a magician coaxing a disappearing act.

WHAT'S ONE THING THAT'S GOING WELL FOR YOU RIGHT NOW?

COURAGEOUS SEED SOWER:

Whisper kind words to yourself, as if planting tiny seeds of courage in the fertile soil of your heart. Watch as they sprout into tall, vibrant affirmations.

SESNORY WONDERLAND:

Use your senses like magic keys, unlocking the wonders of this moment. Touch becomes a velvet touch, sight transforms into a kaleidoscope of colors, and each sound is a symphony.

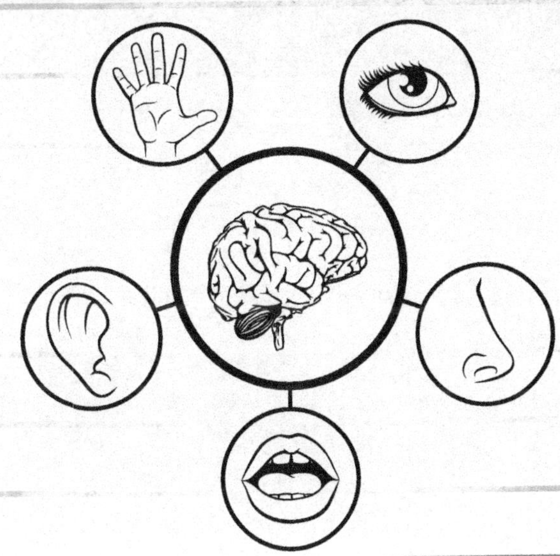

Page of Dreams:

Scribble your worries and dreams upon the pages of your journal. It's like sharing secrets with an old friend who listens without judgment and keeps your dreams safe.

JOYFUL DANCE OF THE HEART:

Dance, jump, or skip for an hour, letting joy and sweat wash away worries. Feel your heart giggle and your worries waltz away.

DRAGON WARNING:

Beware the caffeine and sugar dragons, for they can stir a storm within you. Keep their fiery temper in check, and your peace will reign.

NATURE'S FEAST FIESTA:

Feast on nature's canvas - fruits, vegetables, whole grains, and lean dreams. Let each bite be a brushstroke painting a masterpiece of nourishment.

SLUMBER'S TAPESTRY:

Nestle in slumber's embrace, where dreams are threads weaving a tapestry of restoration and renewal. Each dream a stitch, crafting a quilt of tranquility.

COMPANIONSHIP CARAVEN:

Connect with friends and family, creating an emotional tapestry woven with their support. Each conversation a thread, adding vibrant hues to your heart's design.

GINGERBREAD GALAXY: A COSMIC COCOA DIP

Fetch yourself a gingerbread pal, a biscuit in the shape of a sprightly man (that is, if cinnamon or vanilla tickles your fancy). Lower it with care into a cup brimming with warm cocoa, as if you're sending it on a grand cosmic voyage. You see, my friend, that frothy lava resembles a universe spun with hopes and dreams, gleaming like stars. With each deliberate dip, take a nibble and savor it - a scrumptious dance of flavors and aspirations in your mouth.

TIME-TRAVEL MAESTRO:

Imagine yourself a time-traveling conductor. organizing your tasks like notes in a symphony. Prioritize to harmonize your days and reduce the clamor of overwhelm.

THOUGHT DETECTIVE ADVENTURE:

Embark on a quest as the brave thought detective, unmasking irrational thoughts that sneak into your mind. Each debunked thought is a clue leading to serenity.

SANCTUARY OF SERENITY:

Voyage to a cerebral sanctuary, where you immerse yourself in pastimes such as reading, enjoying music, or indulging in a soothing bath. Allow these interludes to be soothing bubbles that dissolve stress away.

HAVEN OF IMAGINATION:

Close your eyes and imagine a tranquil haven, a place where worries dare not tread. Let your imagination paint peace onto your heart's canvas.

GOAL WEAVING KITTENS:

Like a skilled kitten, break down larger tasks into threads of manageable steps. Weave them together to craft a tapestry of achievement that drapes over your worries.

NEWS NAVIGATOR'S QUEST:

Navigate the seas of news with the wisdom of a seasoned sailor. Limit your exposure to stormy negativity and steer your ship toward calmer waters.

NORTH (5 THINGS YOU SEE) LOOK AROUND AND IDENTIFY FIVE THINGS YOU CAN SEE IN YOUR CURRENT ENVIRONMENT TAKE A MOMENT TO OBSERVE THEIR COLORS, SHAPES, AND DETAILS.

EAST (4 THINGS YOU HEAR) LISTEN CAREFULLY AND NOTICE FOUR THINGS YOU CAN HEAR AROUND YOU. IT COULD BE THE SOUND OF BIRDS, TRAFFIC, PEOPLE TALKING, OR ANY OTHER SOUNDS IN YOUR SURROUNDINGS.

SOUTH (3 THINGS YOU FEEL) PAY ATTENTION TO THREE THINGS YOU CAN PHYSICALLY FEEL. IT MIGHT BE THE TEXTURE OF YOUR CLOTHING, THE SENSATION OF YOUR FEET ON THE GROUND, OR THE WARMTH OF SUNLIGHT ON YOUR SKIN.

WEST (2 THINGS YOU SMELL) FOCUS ON TWO THINGS YOU CAN SMELL. IT COULD BE THE SCENT OF [illegible] FLOWERS, OR ANY OTHER SMELLS IN YOUR VICINITY.

NURTURING
EVERY
SENSATION
WITHIN

USING THIS GROUNDING TECHNIQUE, YOU ENGAGE YOUR SENSES TO BRING YOUR ATTENTION TO THE PRESENT MOMENT AND CONNECT WITH YOUR IMMEDIATE ENVIRONMENT. IT'S A SIMPLE WAY TO ANCHOR YOURSELF AND PROMOTE MINDFULNESS.

☐

KINDNESS COMPANION:

Treat yourself with kindness and understanding. like you would a dear friend. Let self-compassion be the companion that walks beside you through every storm and sunrise.

ROUTINE SYMPHONY:

Picture routine as a conductor's baton, orchestrating predictability in your life's symphony. Let each note of your schedule create harmony and a soothing rhythm.

CREATE CANVAS ADVENTURES:

Dive into creative activities like an explorer of your inner world. Let art, music, and writing be the trails you follow to the treasure trove of therapeutic expression.

POSITIVE TALK MAGICIAN:

Be a magician of words, swapping negativity for encouraging enchantments. With each phrase, conjure self-belief and see how the magic of positivity changes your perspective.

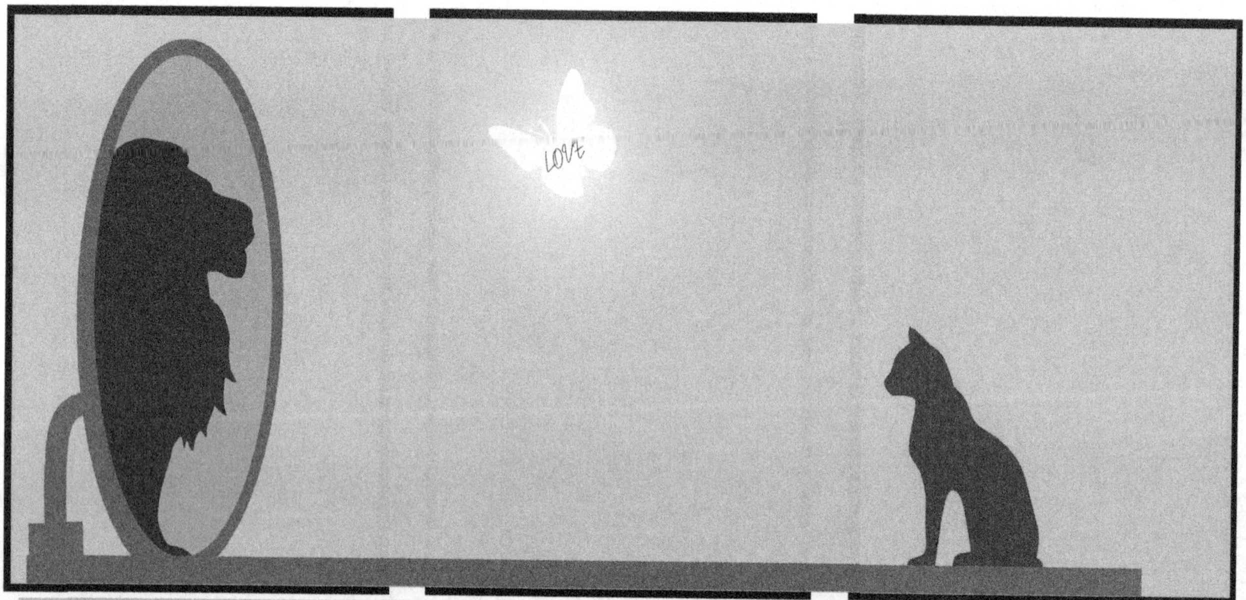

HOLD UP THE MIRROR OF REALITY TO YOUR THOUGHTS, EXAMINING THEIR ACCURACY AND SHATTERING ANY DISTORTED REFLECTIONS.

SCREEN CURTAIN'S CLOSE:

Before bedtime, lower the screen curtain, dimming the electronic glow. Let this be your cue for dreams, as the stage of slumber welcomes its star.

GRATITUDE GARDEN:

Cultivate a garden of gratitude, where each flower is a positive aspect of your life. Water them with attention, and watch your perspective bloom with positivity.

FOCUS SHIFTER:

Like a lens, focus on others' needs through the act of volunteering. It's like adjusting the camera of your heart to capture the bigger picture.

HOBBY KALEIDOSCOPE:

Engage in hobbies as if spinning a colorful kaleidoscope of accomplishment and joy. Each turn reveals a new pattern of satisfaction.

HEART CONVERSATIONS:

Share your thoughts with a counselor, friend, or wise teacher. Like heart-to-heart conversations, their insights become lanterns that light your way through shadows.

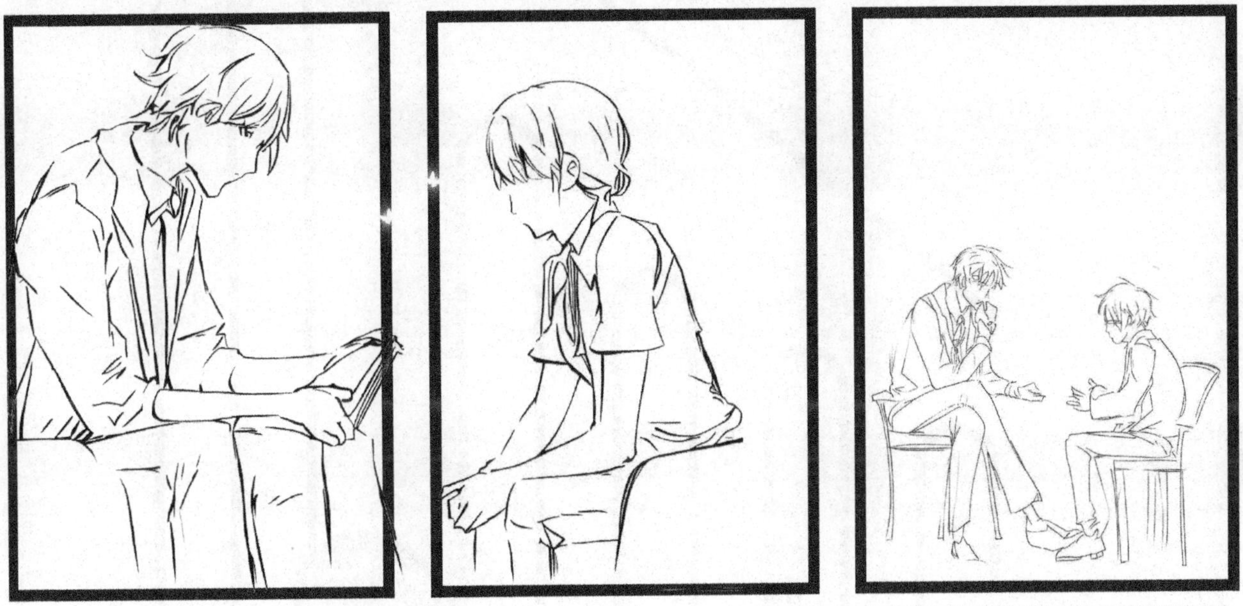

STEP-BY-STEP:

Color in the picture with graded exposure as you embark on a journey, climbing a ladder of anxiety-inducing situations. Each rung is a step towards conquering fears, helping you rise like a valiant knight.

ANXIOUS INK VOYAGE:

Should worry cross your mind this day, ink your concerns in the squares, then sketch them drifting to ocean's floor. Just as paper boats set sail, let time's current guide them astray. Unfurl the next scene, revealing a chest of dreams and hopes untold, each word a precious gem to revive your soul.

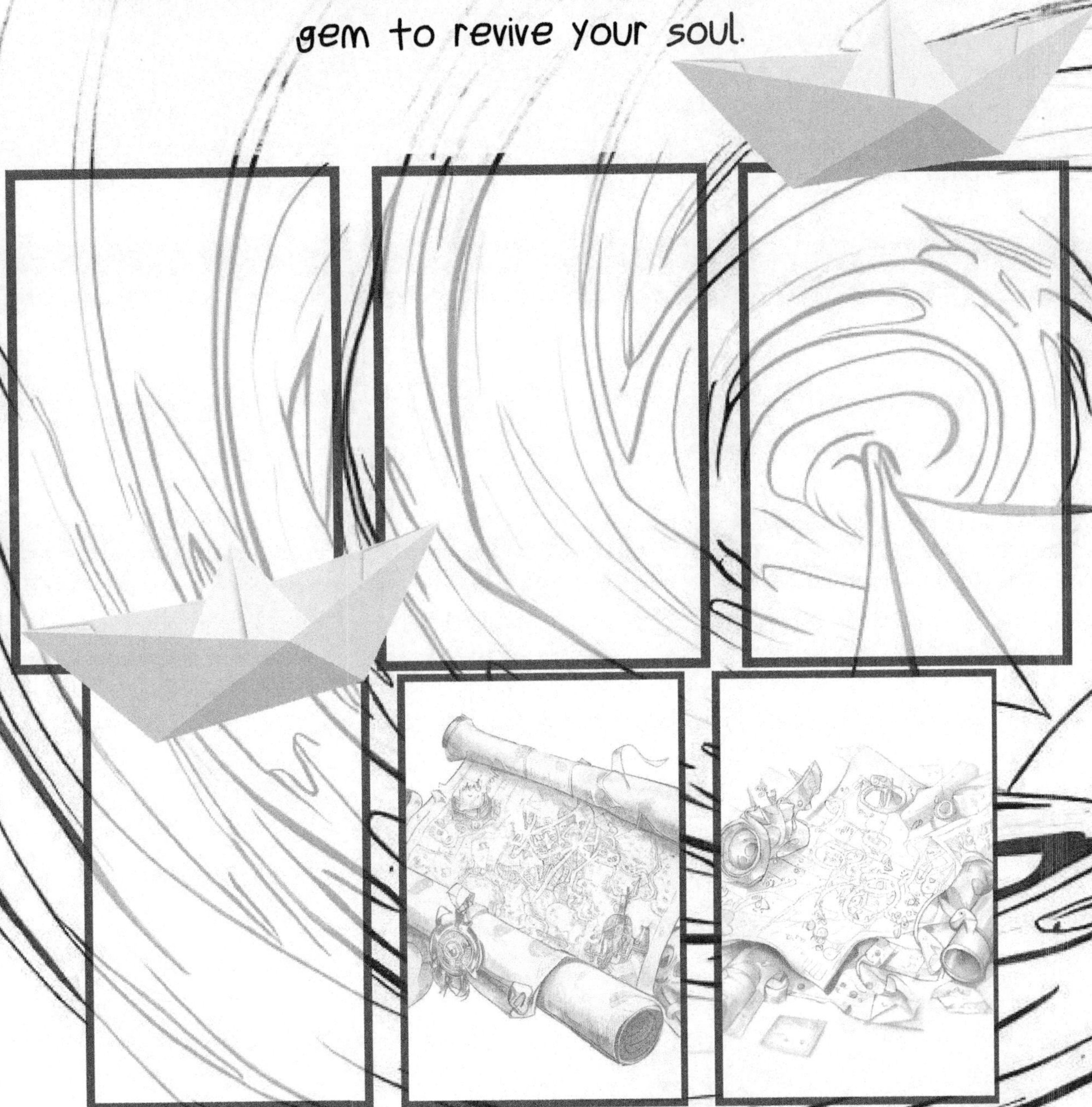

GIGGLE BREEZE:

Participate in activities that tickle your funny bone, such as catching a breeze of laughter, reading a comic or a humorous book, or enjoying a funny film. Let every giggle and smile become a gust that sweeps away clouds of gloom.

THOUGHT WAVES:

Practice acceptance like a beachcomber watching waves arrive and depart. Allow anxious thoughts to wash ashore and recede, without trying to hold or push them away.

HYDRATION HARMONY:

Keep your well-being as lush as a rainforest by staying hydrated. Drink water like sips of life, ensuring anxiety's flames are quenched.

PALETTE OF TRANSFORMATION:

Painting Emotions in Tune with Positivity. Play music from diverse cultures like India, Spain, Thailand, Mexico, or China, and let the rhythm and melody guide your brushstrokes, leading to a unique and expressive masterpiece. In this creative strategy, paint while listening to music you wouldn't normally choose, allowing the melodies to dictate colors, patterns, and emotions in your artwork. This fosters a sensory and imaginative experience.

EMOTION NAMING & TAMING:

When those tricky feelings of fear or anger pay you a visit, give them a jolly name. Let them know they're spotted! Now, be a clever adventurer - step away a bit and see if they're as true as they claim. Sometimes they're just fleeting phantoms, not grand truths. Naming them helps keep their antics in check.

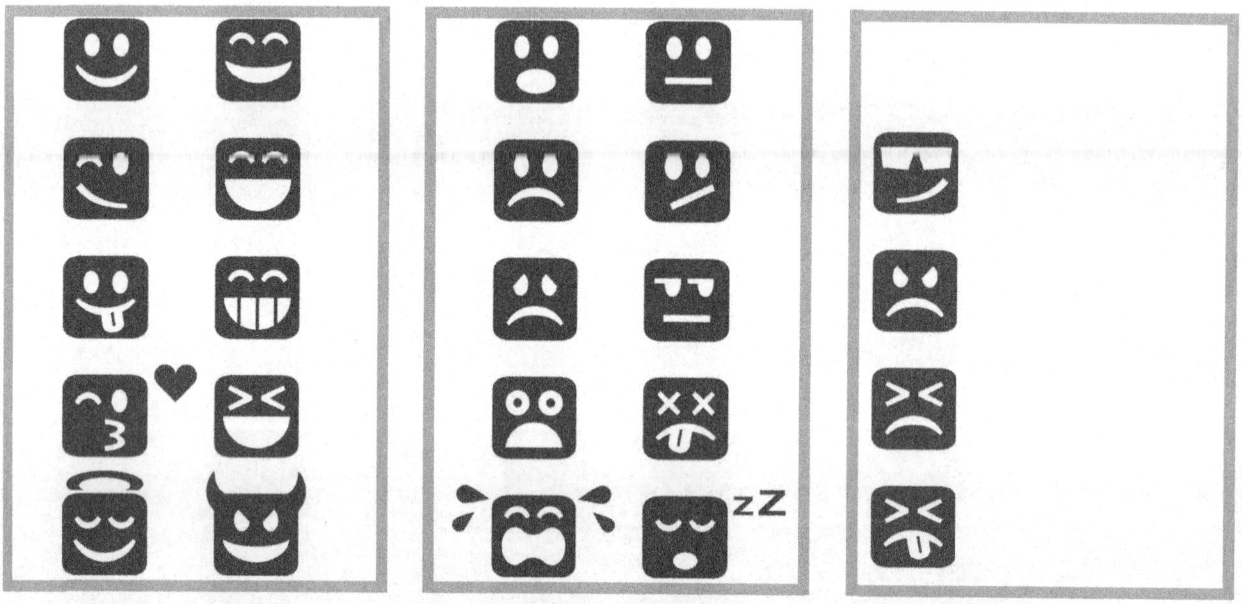

MINDFUL WANDERER:

Walk mindfully, as if exploring an enchanted forest. Feel the earth's pulse with each step, and let the rhythm of your breath guide you through the woods of thoughts.

CONFIDENCE TAPESTRY:

Craft attainable goals, akin to weaving a tapestry of accomplishment. Observe your progress, thread by thread, crafting a masterpiece that nurtures confidence. Set targets that are Smart, Measurable, Achievable, Realistic, and Targeted.

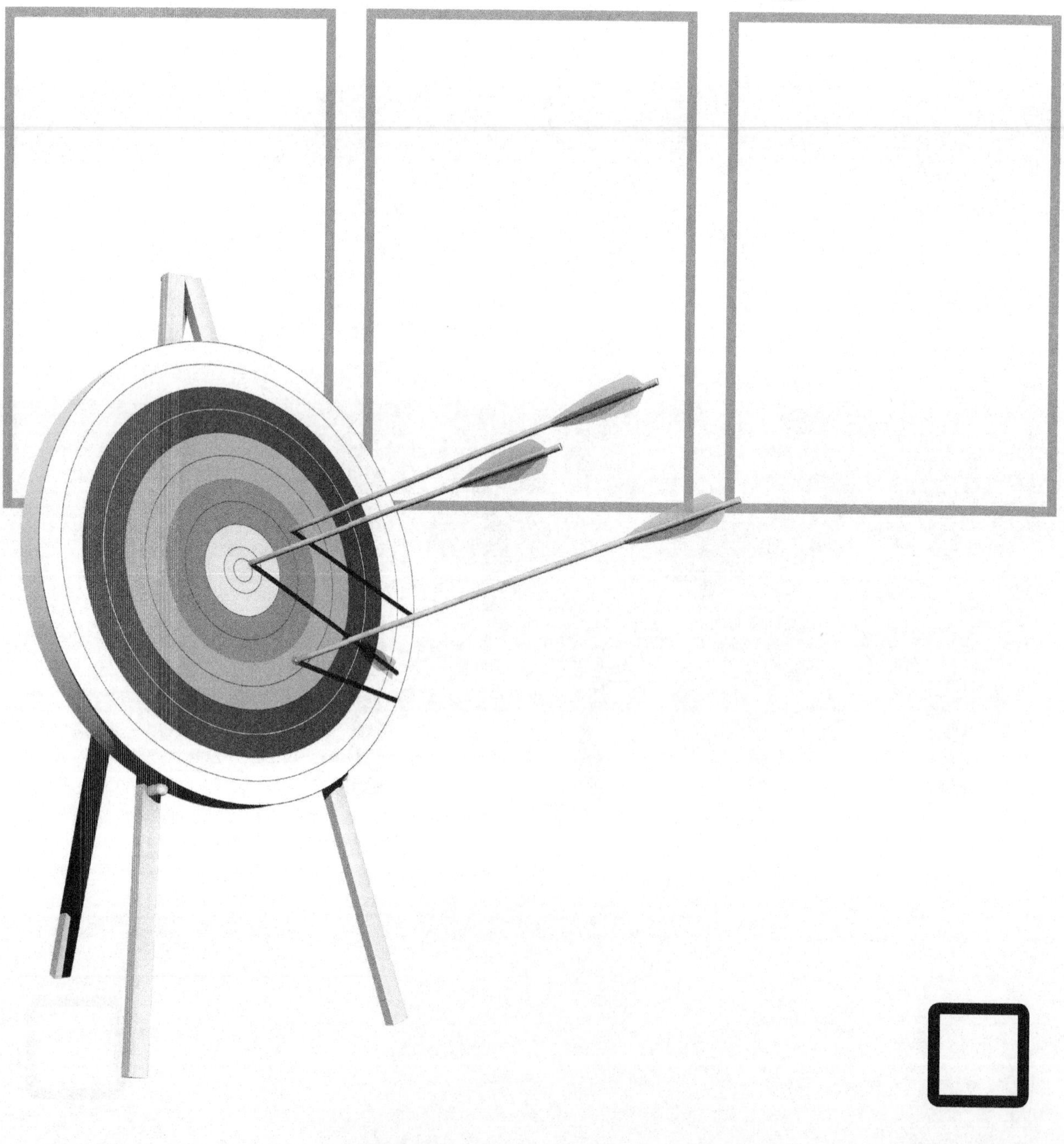

HERBAL HARMONY:

Sip herbal teas like a potion of relaxation. Chamomile and valerian root, like nature's lullabies, sing you into a peaceful slumber.

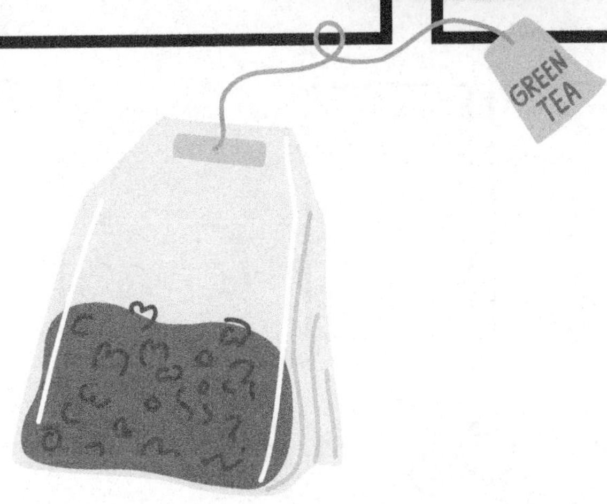

SELF-CARE SYMPHONY:

Engage in self-care as if composing a harmonious melody for your well-being. Activities like baths and self-massage become notes that soothe your soul's song.

BOUNDARY SCULPTOR:

Shape boundaries like an artist crafting a masterpiece. Learn to say no to commitments that strain your canvas. ensuring your creation remains vibrant and serene.

HAND OF COMPASSION:

Draw around your hand and and then draw the things that make you happy within the hand. It's a great way to remind yourself of the things that bring joy to your life.

CALM THROUGH THE SQUEEZE:

Transform tension with the touch of stress balls or fidget toys. As you squeeze, release and transmute anxiety in exchange for soothing calm.

ANIMAL AFFECTION INTERLUDE:

Spend time with animals as if sharing a gentle interlude. Let their presence soothe your spirit, and feel the threads of connection weave around your heart.

EXPRESSIVE CANVAS VOYAGE:

Engage in art, writing, or music like embarking on a colorful voyage. Let creativity be your ship, navigating emotions and thoughts to shores of positivity.

MINDFUL BREATHING:

Picture this - you're sipping from a cup of calmness and breathing out all that pesky tension. Whenever anger or fear show up uninvited, pause like a wise old owl and take a deep, slow breath. Imagine you're sipping tranquility and blowing away worries. This magical breath calms the storm and lets your thoughts find their balance.

CLASSICAL GUIDANCE:

Use guided relaxation like following a path of tranquility. Let classical recordings be your compass, leading you through serene landscapes of calm.

COUNTDOWN PALETTE:

Fill the 54321 countdown box with tranquil hues. like a painter's brush sweeping calming shades across your canvas of thoughts.

5

4

3

2

1

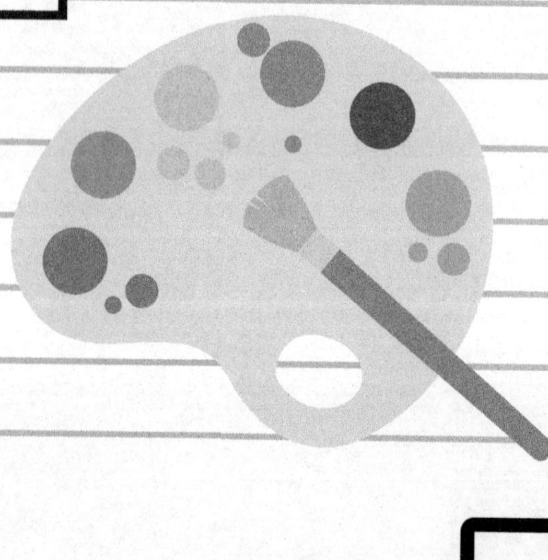

TREE OF REFLECTION:

Today, visit a tree, examining its textures and colors. Just as our bodies hide complex systems, imagine if our forms were transparent - we'd resemble walking trees, intricate and fascinating.

JAR OF MEMORIES:

Find a jar and start filling it with splendid memories - slips of paper adorned with enchanting words, clippings from magazines, a pebble, a shell, a toy. This, my dear reader, is your wondrous memory jar, a vessel for treasured tales.

EMERALD EMBRACE:

Walk barefoot on grass, allowing its touch to become a soothing embrace. Feel the earth's pulse beneath your feet, grounding you in nature's comforting arms.

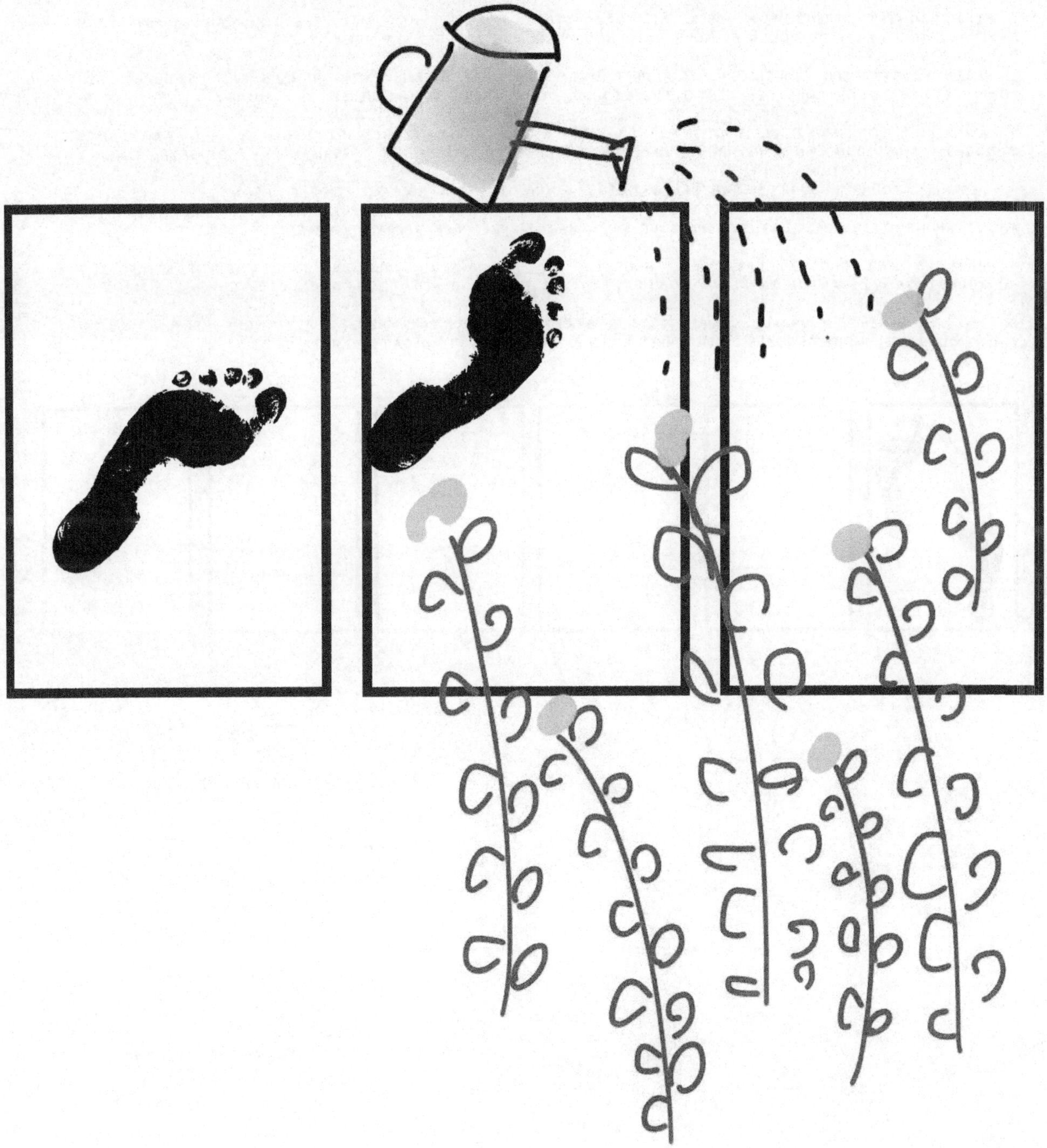

GRASS LAND BALLET:

BALLET BAREFOOT ON THE GRASS, WHICH NOT ONLY RECONNECTS YOU WITH NATURE BUT ALSO GROUNDS YOU IN THE PRESENT MOMENT. THE ACT OF REFRAMING YOUR THOUGHTS DURING THIS PRACTICE CAN PROMOTE A MORE POSITIVE AND BALANCED MINDSET

1. FIND A QUIET GREEN SPACE: SEEK OUT A PEACEFUL SPOT IN NATURE WHERE YOU CAN SAFELY WALK BAREFOOT ON GRASS. IT COULD BE YOUR GARDEN, A PARK, OR ANY GRASSY AREA.

2. BEGIN YOUR BAREFOOT WALK: AS YOU STEP ONTO THE GRASS, FEEL THE COOLNESS AND TEXTURE UNDER YOUR FEET. LET YOUR TOES SINK INTO THE GROUND, CONNECTING WITH THE EARTH'S ENERGY.

3. AWARENESS OF NEGATIVE THOUGHTS: AS YOU WALK, ACKNOWLEDGE ANY NEGATIVE OR WORRISOME THOUGHTS THAT COME TO MIND. UNDERSTAND THAT THESE THOUGHTS ARE A NORMAL PART OF BEING HUMAN.

4. REFRAME YOUR THOUGHTS: WHILE WALKING, CONSCIOUSLY REFRAME THESE NEGATIVE THOUGHTS. CHALLENGE THEM WITH MORE POSITIVE OR REALISTIC PERSPECTIVES. FOR EXAMPLE, IF YOU'RE WORRIED ABOUT AN UPCOMING MEETING, REMIND YOURSELF THAT YOU'RE PREPARED AND CAPABLE.

5. BREATHE AND GROUND: TAKE DEEP BREATHS AS YOU WALK, INHALING THE FRESHNESS OF THE SURROUNDINGS. VISUALIZE INHALING POSITIVITY AND EXHALING NEGATIVITY.

6. FEEL THE BENEFITS: AS YOU COMPLETE YOUR GRASS-WALK, NOTICE THE SHIFT IN YOUR MENTAL STATE. YOU SHOULD FEEL MORE GROUNDED, CENTERED, AND LESS BURDENED BY NEGATIVE THOUGHTS..

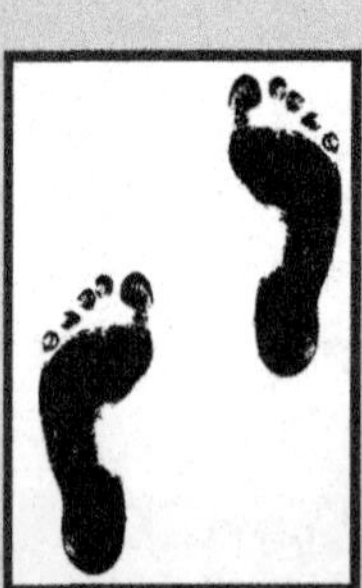

HERBAL CALM CHRONICLES:

Delve into herbal supplements as if exploring a garden of tranquility. Some herbs like ashwagandha and passionflower might hold the secret to soothing breezes within.

CLEAR SKIES CONVERSATION:

Practice talking just like you're sending a soft breeze through the clear blue skies of understanding. Make your words the gentle winds that blow away the clouds of confusion.

SENSORY ANCHORING:

Use sensory experiences like holding an ice cube or touching textures as if casting an anchor to the present moment. Let each sensation be a tether grounding you in now.

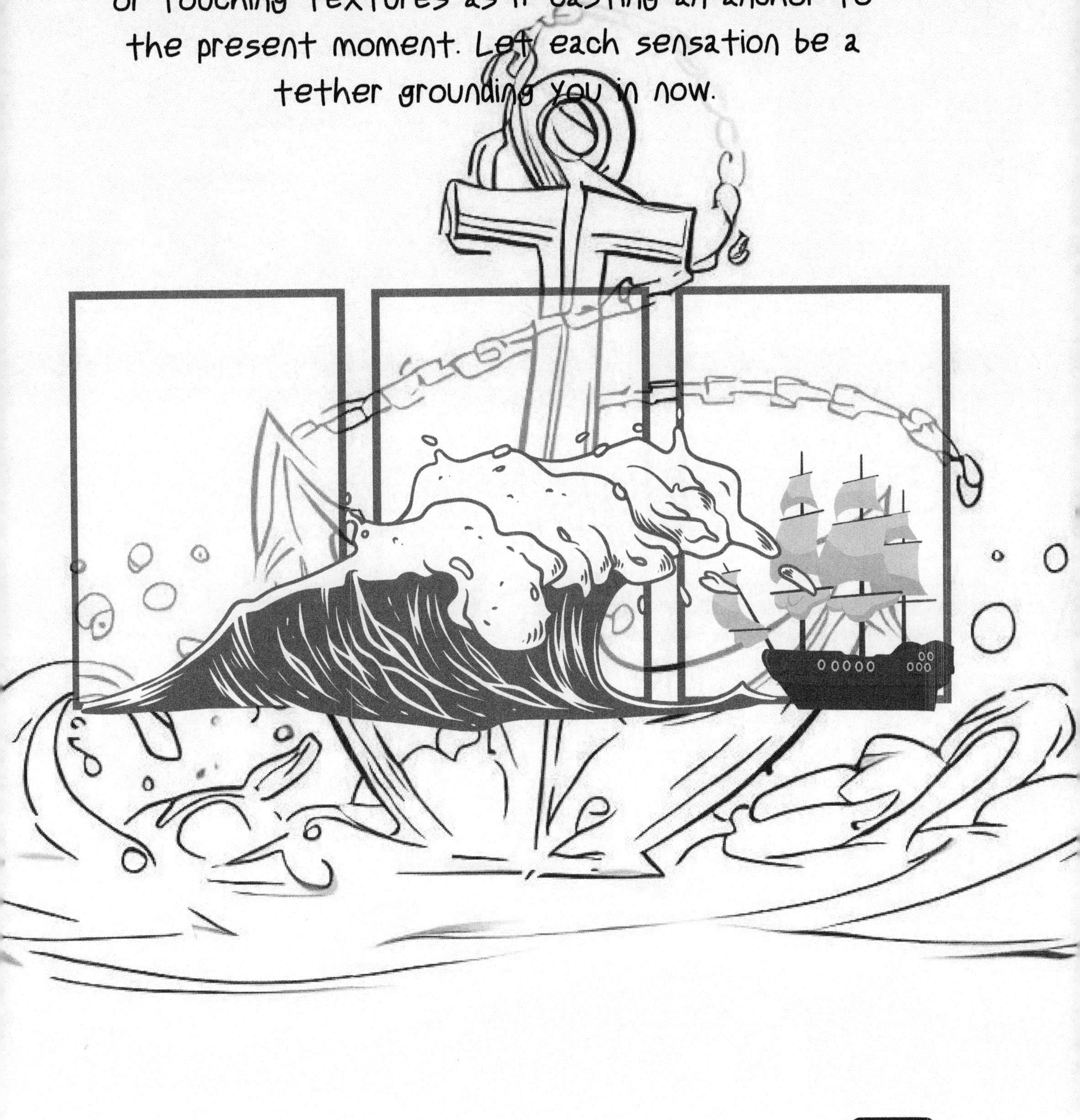

SILENCE OASIS:

Seek refuge in quiet environments, as if discovering hidden oases. Let silence be your balm, soothing the senses and quieting the clamor of the world.

DESENSITIZATION EXPEDITION:

Embark on a journey to conquer anxiety triggers, just like a courageous explorer. With each step, you become stronger and more resilient, taming the wild beasts of unease. For example, let's consider public speaking: Begin by talking to a mirror, then to a stuffed animal, and gradually progress to speaking in front of a small, familiar group.

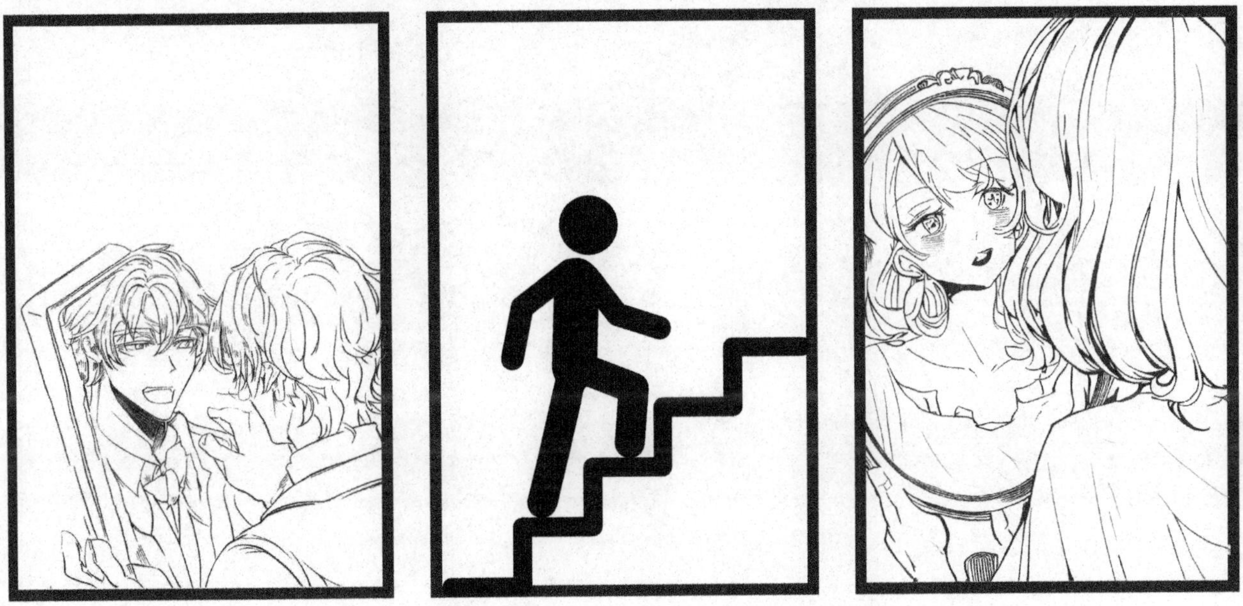

MINDFUL MOVEMENT SYMPHONY:

Immerse yourself in Tai Chi, stretching, or Yoga, just like a conductor guiding a symphony of movement and mindfulness. Each pose becomes a note, harmoniously composing a serene melody that effectively reduces stress.

NATURE'S EMBRACE:

Connect with nature like a reunion with an old friend. Spend time outdoors and engage in activities that mirror the harmony of the natural world.

THOUGHT DISTANCING:

Practice cognitive distancing as if stepping back from a painting. View anxious thoughts like brushstrokes on canvas, realizing they're not the masterpiece of your true self.

(Cognitive dissonance is when you feel kind of uncomfortable in your mind because you have two ideas that don't match, like if you know you should eat healthy but you really want to eat a lot of candy. It's like having a little argument inside your head about what you should do)

COMMUNITY BONDING VOYAGE:

Engage in community activities as if sailing on a ship of shared interests. Let the camaraderie of clubs and groups become a lighthouse in the sea of social support.

FLUTTERING EMBRACE:

Give yourself a butterfly hug, enveloping yourself in gentle taps like the fluttering embrace of a butterfly's wings. For 30 seconds, let this act be a soothing whisper of care.

DIGITAL SERENITY PATH:

Navigate technology mindfully, as if walking a serene trail. Set time limits, and with each interaction, practice mindfulness, ensuring the digital realm remains a tranquil haven.

EMOTION NAMING:

Amidst the storm of feelings, utter the names of your negative emotions. Pause and whisper their names, then reverse-engineer them to understand their source.

JOURNAL OF ECHOING HEARTS:

Journal as if your heart's whispers are ink on paper. Let your emotions pour like stories, revealing their hidden chapters and weaving threads of insight.

BREATH'S CALMING OXYGEN:

Breathe in and out as if sipping from a cup of calmness. When strong feelings come, take a moment to breathe, and let each breath make those feelings less sharp and soothe your mind.

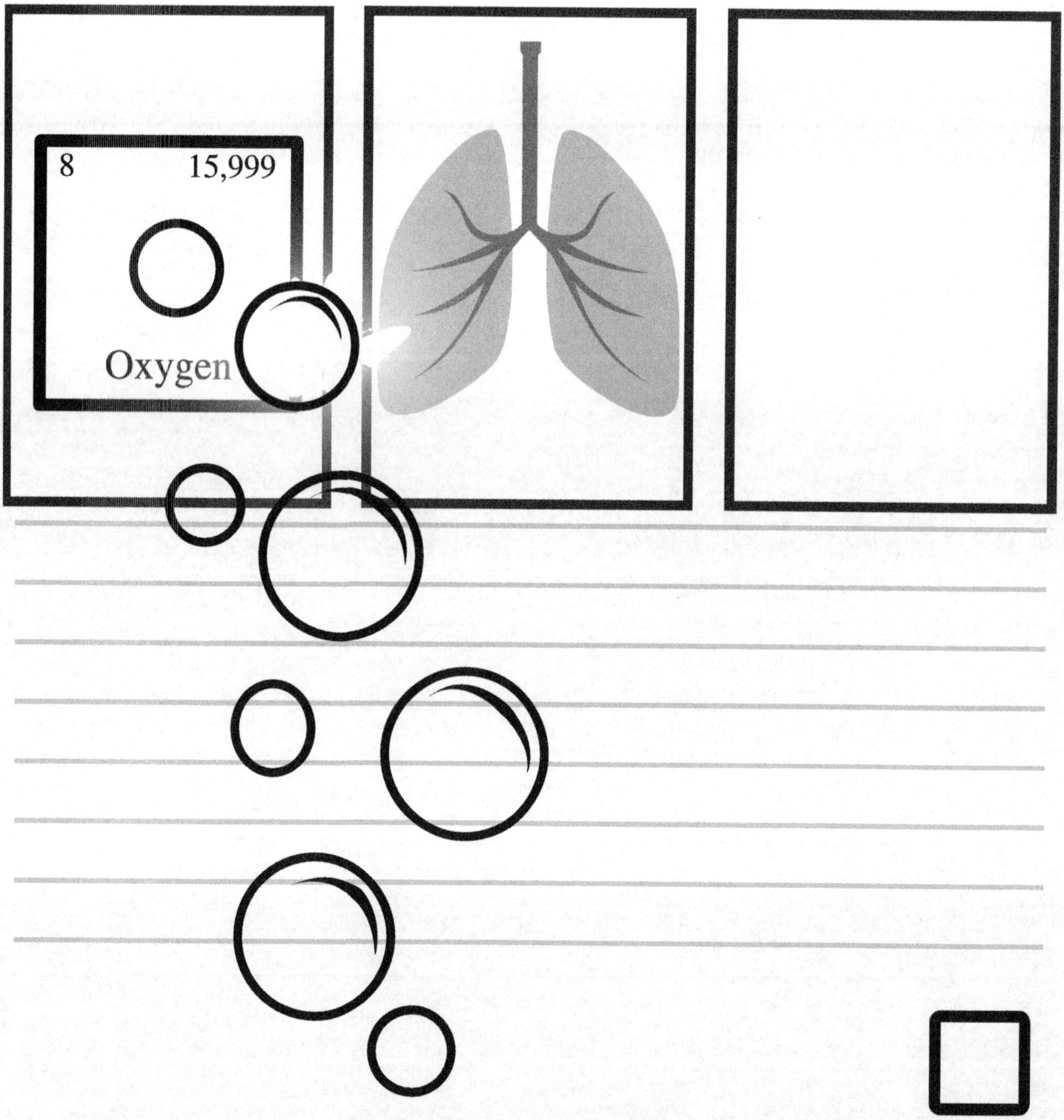

ATMOSPHERE READING:

Before emotional storms, read the atmosphere like a weathered sailor. Understand the currents of context, ensuring reactions are guided by clear skies of understanding.

TRANSFORMING THOUGHTS:

Imagine turning tricky negative thoughts into puzzles that can change shape. then reshape them into positive stories that shine like sunlight.

METAPHORIC VISUALIZATIONS:

Imagine your fears and angers as fluffy clouds or tiny leaves dancing on a river's surface. Watch them float away, carried by the winds and currents. Just like an artist painting with whimsy, you're reshaping your view of those emotions. They become less like giants and more like friendly drifters.

MINDFUL PRESENCE:

Walk the path of mindfulness, where each step is a brushstroke of the present, painting over emotions' stormy clouds.

THEAPEUTIC EXPLORATIONS:

seek guidance from wise counselors or advisors. who can help you unravel the mysteries of emotions and navigate their intricate paths.

BOUNDARIES OF RESPECT:

Set personal boundaries, like fences around your emotional garden, protecting it from the storms of life.

FRIENDSHIP HAVEN:

Seek solace in companionship, sharing the burden of emotions with friends, family, or kindred spirits.

SELF-CARE OASIS:

Dedicate time to your well-being, tending to your spirit with rest, nourishment, and activities that bring joy.

THOUGHT PUZZLES:

Tackle those pesky negative thoughts like tricky riddles. and twist them into delightful tales of positivity.

IDENTIFY TRIGGERS:

Detect the sources of emotional storms. like skilled navigators charting rough waters to find safe passages.

EMOTIONAL EXPRESSIONS:

Express your feelings through words, art, or other creative outlets, like a storyteller sharing tales of the heart.

THOUGHT SHIFTS:

Transform negative thoughts into positive ones. like a word artist rearranging letters to craft uplifting sentences.

STORYBOOK TECHNIQUE:

Picture this - you're the author of your own story! Grab your pencil or crayons and draw a funny comic strip or write a tale. Turn those tricky situations that bring out fear or anger into a wild adventure. Change the characters, give them new names, and let the story unfold in giggles. By spinning tales, you change the real-world game.

RELAXATION RITUALS:

Practice calming rituals such as deep breaths and visualization, conjuring a sense of tranquility.

ACTIVITY ENERGIES:

Engage in regular physical activity. as if you're recharging your emotional batteries with joyful movement.

DREAMFUL SLUMBER:

Embrace a peaceful sleep for at least 8 hours each night, where dreams stitch together the threads of your emotions, preparing you for a new beginning with each sunrise.

WHISPERS OF A LEAF:

Place a leaf gently down, my friend, and give it a closer look. Study its delicate veins, the hues it wears, the textures that tell its tale. Jot down your observations, the secrets it whispers, and the feelings it stirs within your heart.

GRATITUDE ATTITUDE:

Foster a heart of thankfulness, akin to a collector cherishing rare and beautiful treasures.

FEED THE DUCKS:

Off you go to the quacking pond, armed with slices of bread, to treat the waddling ducks with their feathery company.

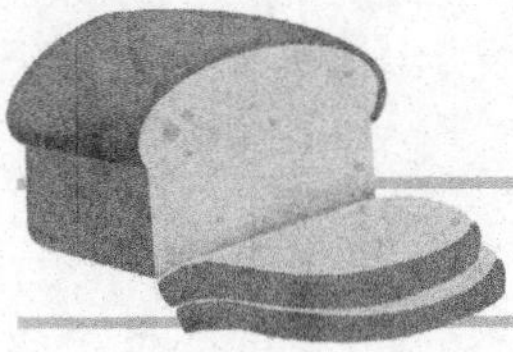

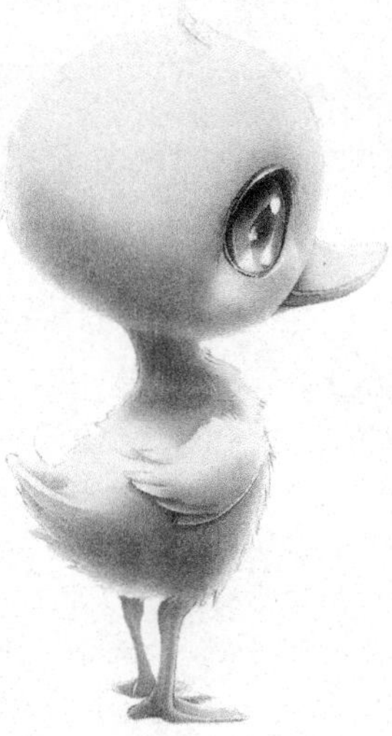

Connect with like-hearted individuals, forming bonds that stand strong in the face of emotional storms.

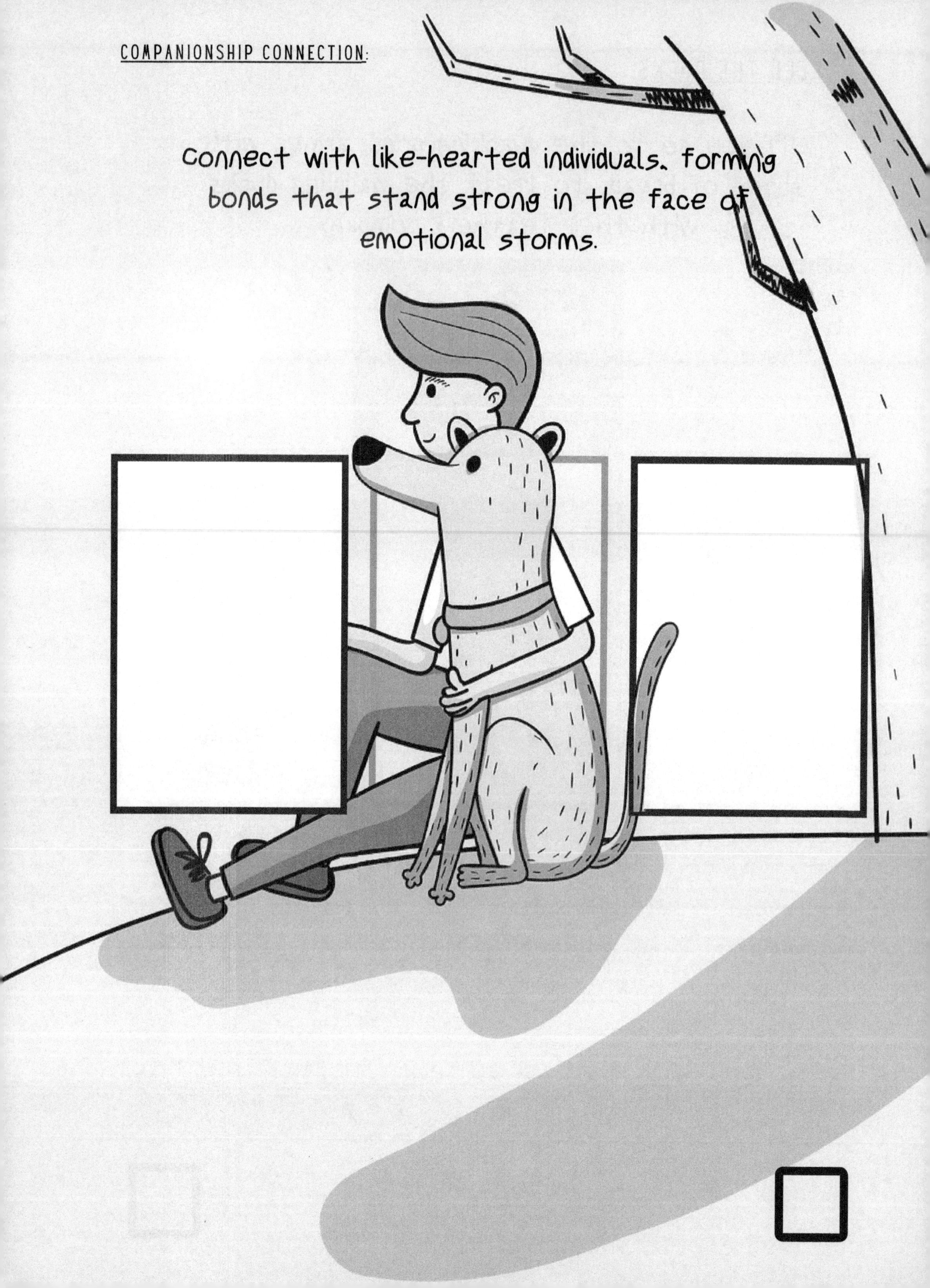

FORGIVING PATHS:

Practice forgiveness, akin to a traveler releasing heavy burdens along the path to peace, start with yourself.

MOMENTS OF RESPITE:

Take breaks to rest and rejuvenate, as if a weary traveler stops to savor the view before continuing the journey.

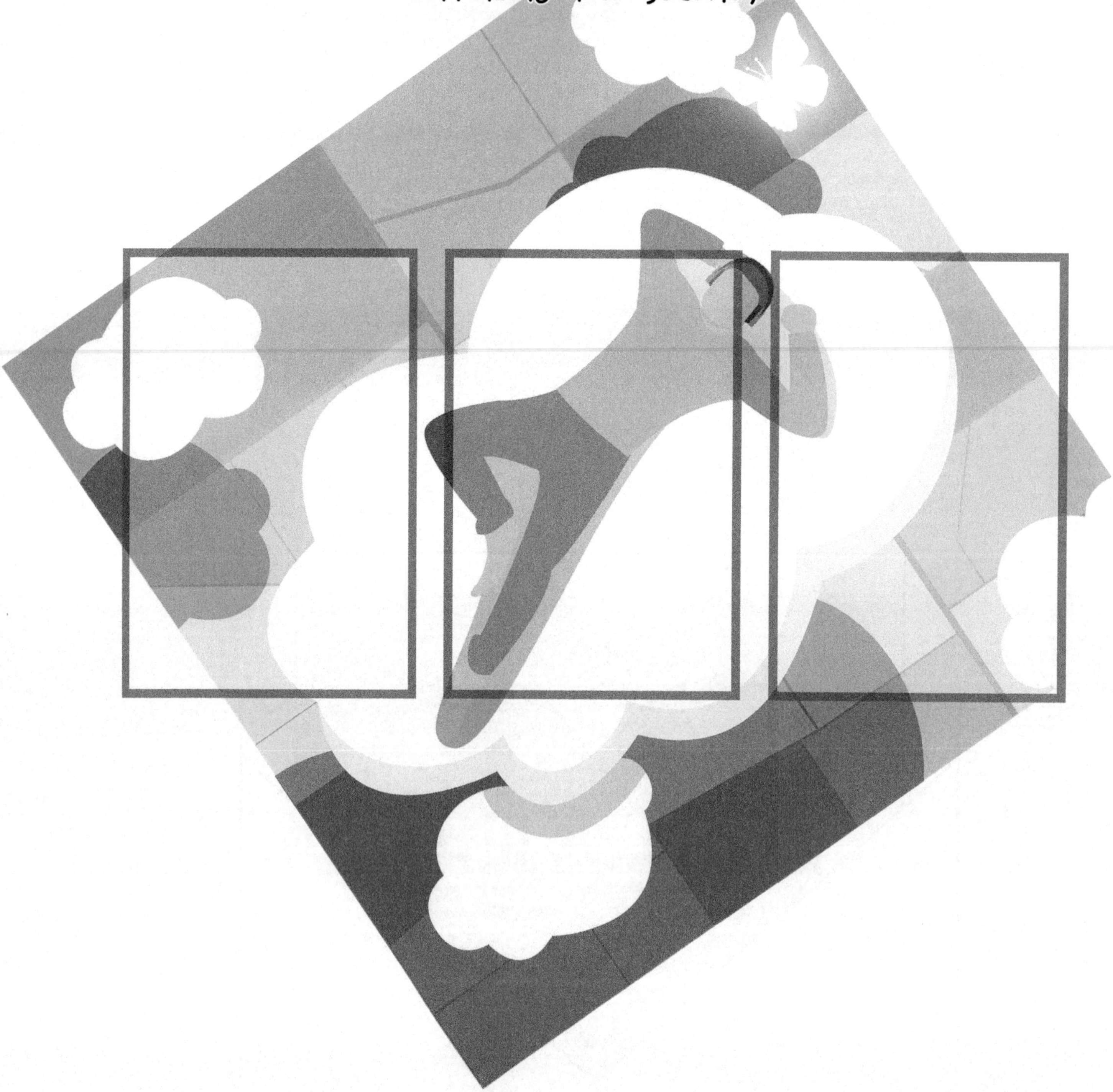

<u>WHOOING HARMONY</u>:

"Oooooooooooooooooooooooooo"

Channel your inner owl, sending ooo sounds into the air like a melodic hoot. This enchanting song sets free the magic of acetylcholine, a wondrous elixir that dances within us, orchestrating the symphony of muscles, memories, and the autonomic dance of nerves.

RAINBOW REFLECTION:

Picture your worries as raindrops falling from the sky. But here's the twist – each drop carries a color, like a rainbow of feelings. Watch them fall, but don't get soaked in them. Let them slide off like water on an umbrella. See how the rainbow of emotions fades away, leaving a clear sky.

GREEN DREAMSCAPE:

Unleash your artistic spirit and paint a vibrant field of green. In the realm of color psychology. green is a soothing balm for eyes weary from the world's hustle. Let your strokes of emerald sweep you into a tranquil reverie.

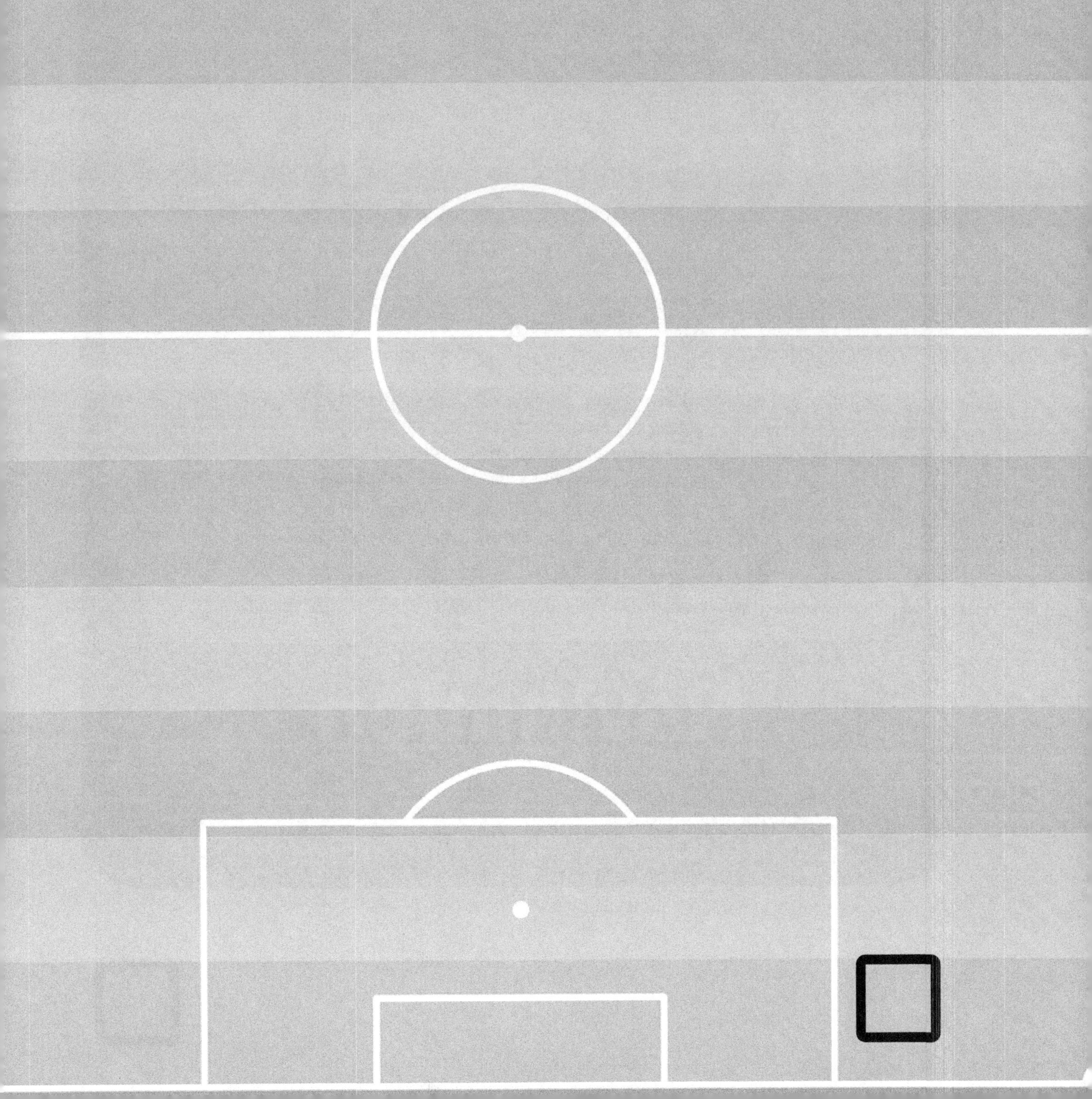

CAPTAIN OF EMOTIONS:

Imagine you're sailing on the sea of emotions. Sometimes stormy waves of fear and anger come your way. But guess what? You're the captain of this ship! Steer through the waves with your anchor of courage and your compass of positivity. Navigate towards the calm shores of understanding.

Navigation

BLUE HORIZON:

Dab your canvas with shades of blue, like the heavens stretching over an open sea. In the realm of color psychology, blue whispers serenity, offering calm waters for the soul to sail and a tapestry of peace for weary eyes.

FLORAL DISCOVERY:

Seek out a delicate flower, a token of nature's beauty. Gently affix it here, like a bookmark in your heart, reminding you of the world's intricate wonders.

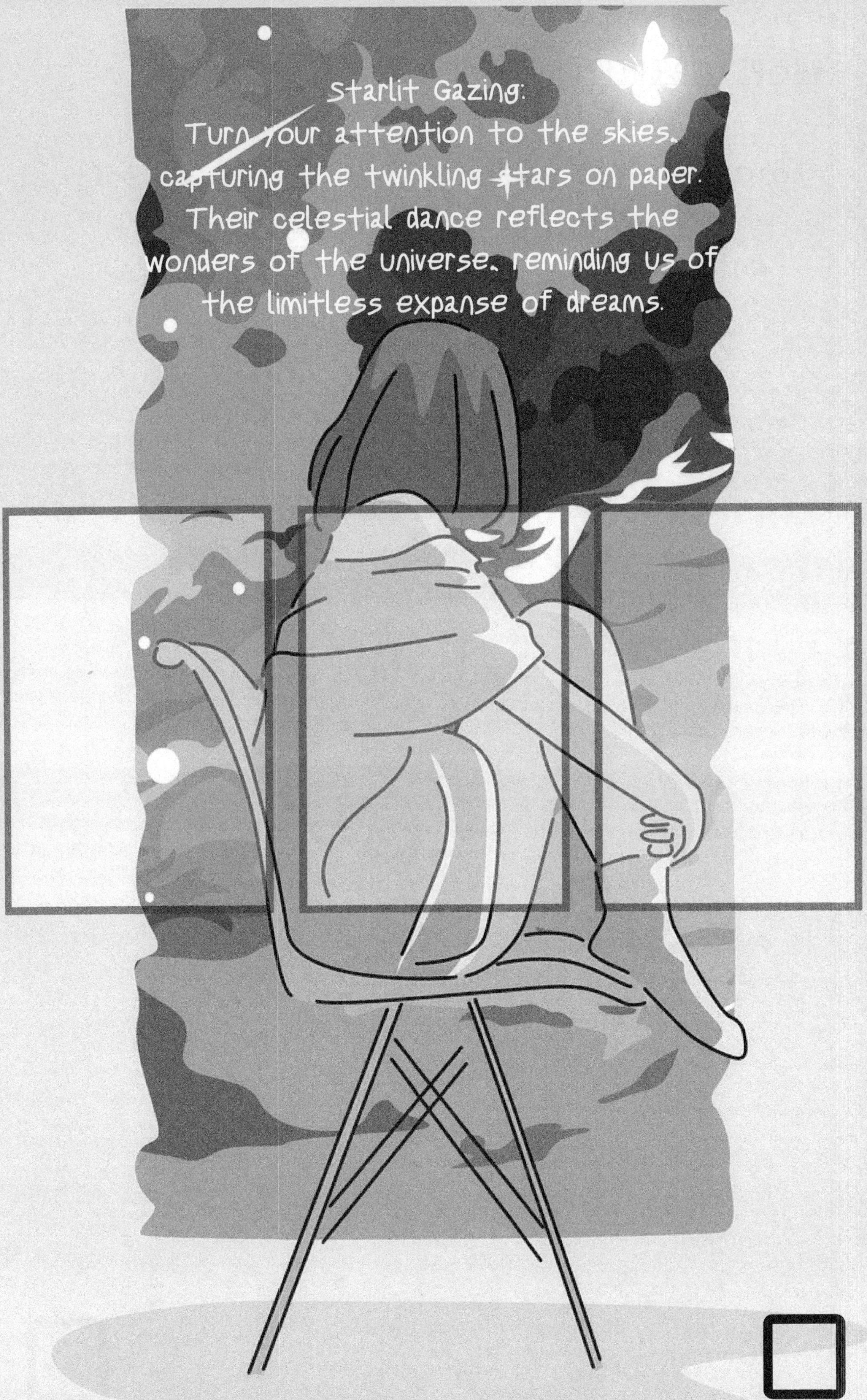
Starlit Gazing:
Turn your attention to the skies, capturing the twinkling stars on paper. Their celestial dance reflects the wonders of the universe, reminding us of the limitless expanse of dreams.

WHISPERING BREEZE:

Close your eyes and listen to the breeze's soft whispers. With your pencil, etch its secrets onto paper, as if you're preserving nature's stories in ink.

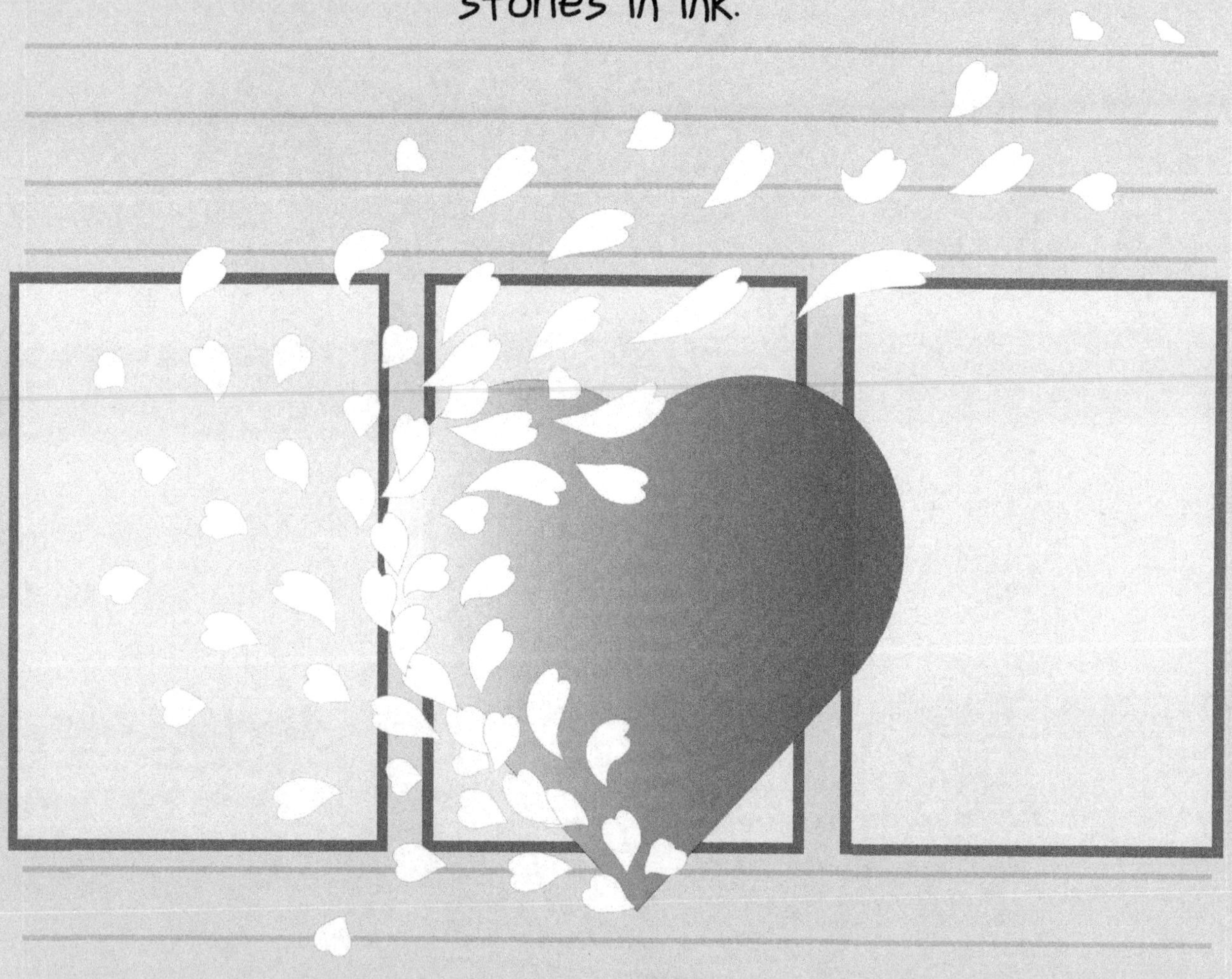

GOLDEN RAYS:

Paint a sunlit landscape, embracing the warmth of golden hues. These rays hold the power to brighten even the darkest corners of your heart, casting out shadows with their radiant touch.

HEARTFELT REFLECTION:

Take a moment to ponder upon your thoughts, feelings, and actions, all wrapped in the warm embrace of understanding. Instead of being harsh on yourself, embark on a gentle exploration of the reasons behind your deeds, like uncovering hidden treasures with a curious heart.

OCEAN'S SERENADE:

With blues and greens, paint an ocean's embrace. As waves meet the shore, imagine your worries receding, carried away by the tides.

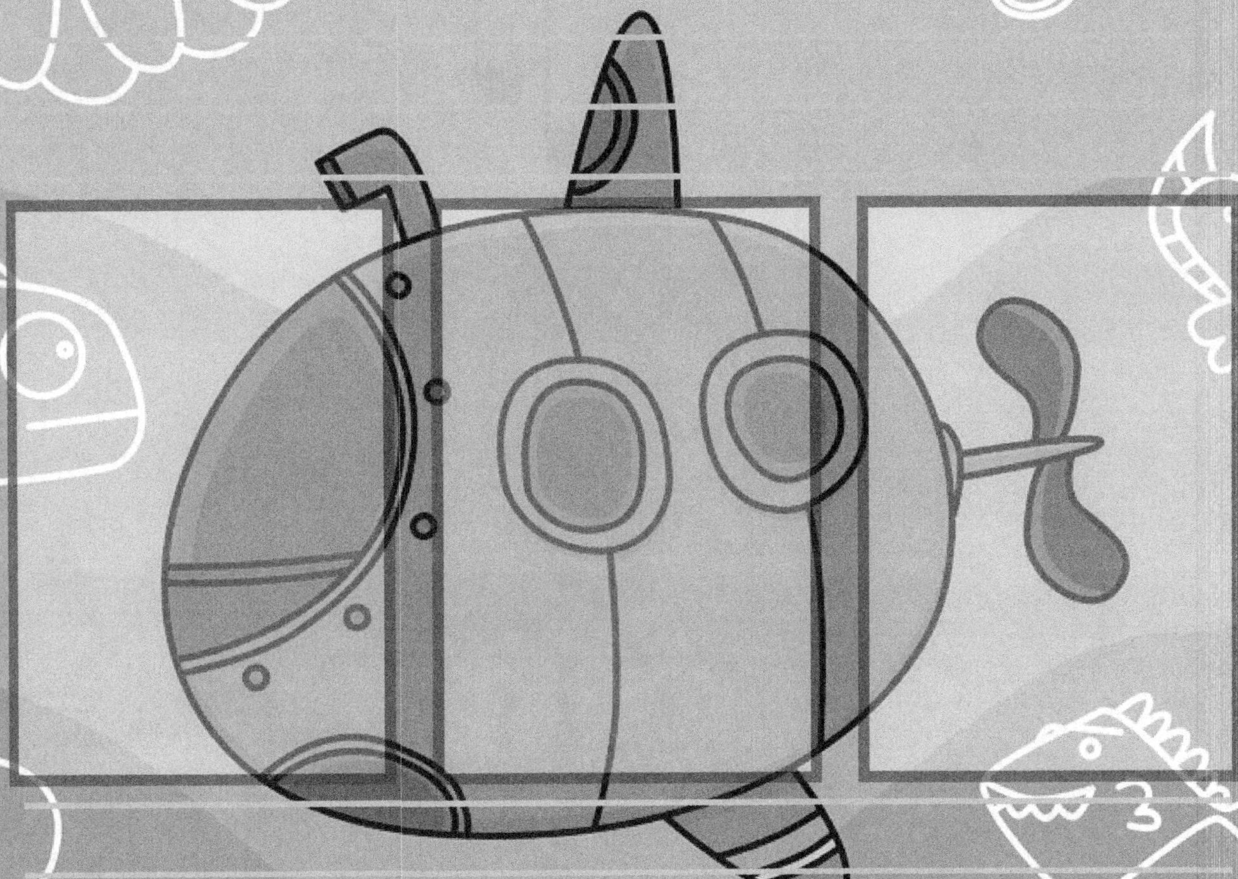

NATURE'S SYMPHONY:

In your mind's eye,
Create a musical scene of nature's orchestra – birds, rustling leaves, and murmuring streams. Let their harmonious melody serenade your spirit.

SUNRISE WHISPERS:

Capture the dawn's first light on paper, as if brushing the sky with the softest strokes of rose and gold. Let this sunrise remind you of the promise of new beginnings.

RAINBOW'S DANCE:

Paint a rainbow arching across the canvas, like a bridge between storms and sunshine. Each color holds a lesson, teaching us to embrace life's spectrum.

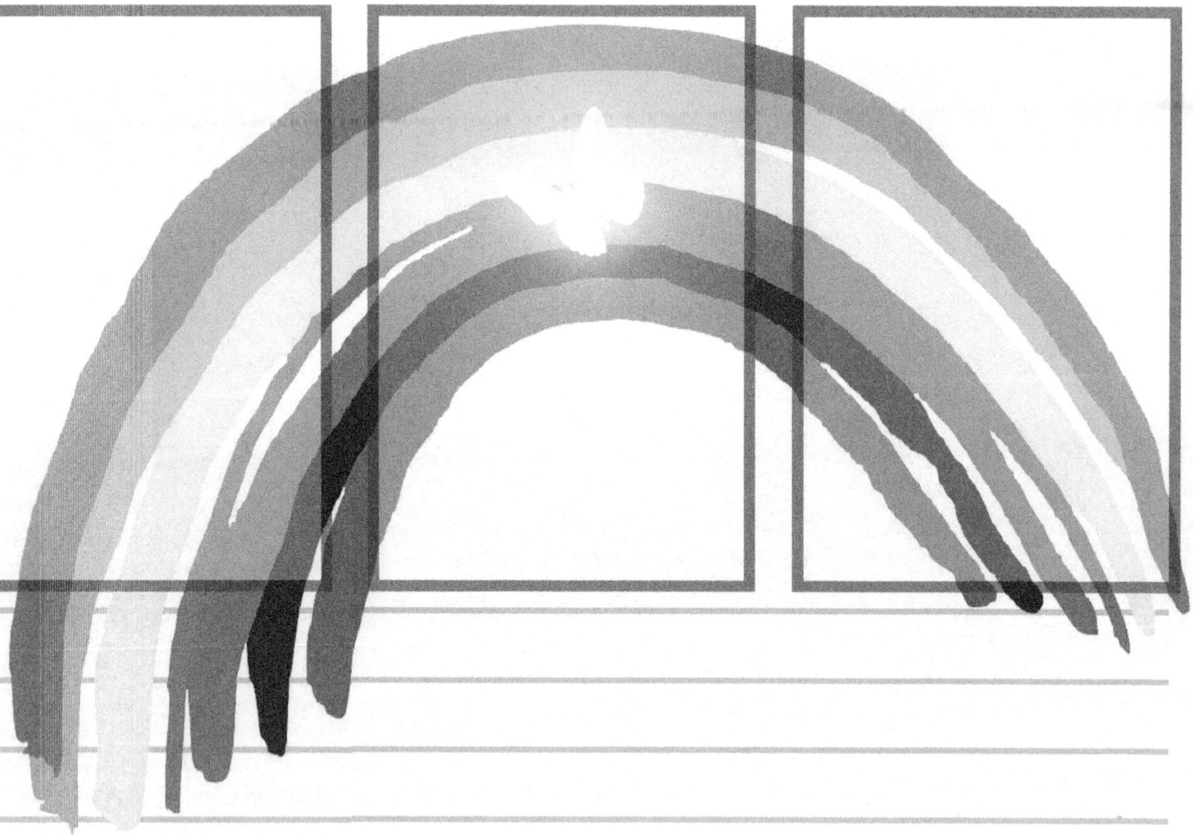

STARRY NIGHT:

Imagine a night sky adorned with stars. and capture this celestial dance with your artistic flair. Let the canvas mirror the universe's twinkling wonders.

WHISPERS OF INSIGHT:

Tune in to the whispers of wisdom within, like leaves rustling secrets in an enchanted forest.

- Example: "In the hush of introspection, the leaves of my thoughts murmured guidance, leading me from the maze of emotions."

FLOWER'S SECRETS

Find a hidden treasure in nature - a delicate flower. Adorn this page with its beauty, a reminder of the wonders that flourish in the world.

SPARKLING SELF-TALK:

Become a wordsmith of positivity, crafting sentences that gently guide your thoughts away from negativity. Pick up a dictionary and unearth a treasure trove of uplifting words and phrases, like "serenity," "radiant," and "inner strength." Create your own affirmations and mantras that resonate with your heart's desires, infusing your inner dialogue with the power of positive language.

COLORFUL PALETTE:

Look around and identify five different colors in your environment. Notice their shades and variations. Using this simple exercise to ground yourself in the here and now.

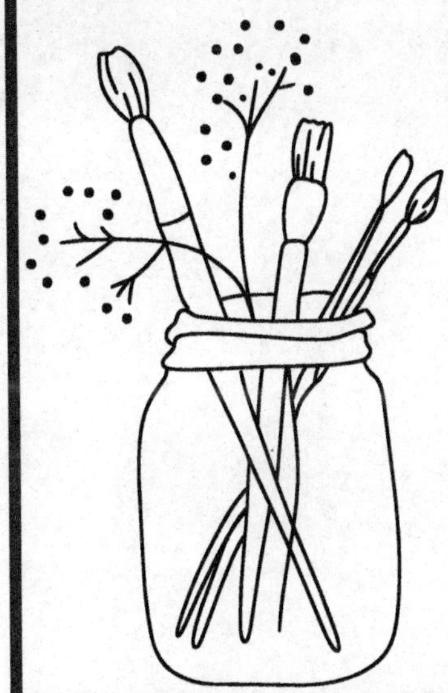

Emotion Explorer:

Delve into your feelings with curiosity, as if you're on a grand adventure through the realm of emotions.

CLOUD CHASER:

Watch emotions like passing clouds.
acknowledging their presence without being
swept up in their storms.

STORYTELLER'S VOYAGE:

Imagine a story and describe five imaginary elements in it. Then, listen for four story-related sounds, feel three emotions connected to the tale, imagine two scents associated with the setting, and picture one pivotal scene.

INNER GARDENER:

Cultivate the garden of your mind, uprooting negative thoughts and nurturing the blooms of positivity.

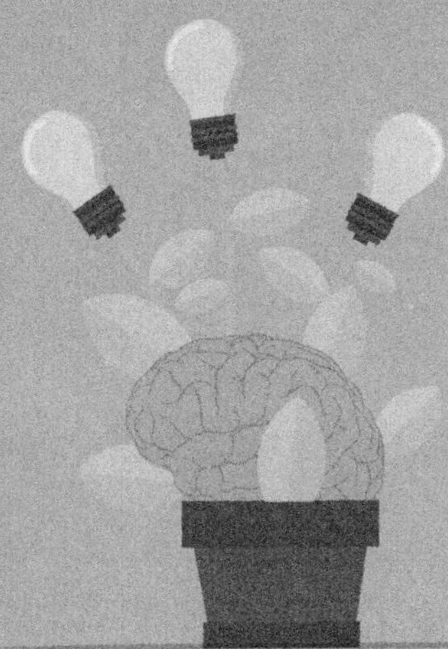

SPEAKING BOOKS:

Choose three books at random and flip through their pages without peeking. After doing so, place your finger on a page, and write down the word or sentence where your finger lands.

BREATHING BEACON:

Close your eyes and take deep, deliberate breaths. Imagine each inhale and exhale as a beam of light that spreads throughout your body, bringing you into a calm and centered state.

TEXTURE EXPLORATION:

Focus on the sensations of different textures around you. Run your fingers over surfaces like wood, fabric, or grass, allowing the tactile experiences to anchor you..

URBAN EXPLORER:

Walk around and spot five signs of urban life. Then, listen for four city sounds, name three different materials you encounter, find two things with contrasting textures, and observe one aspect of nature amidst the urban setting.

ARTISTIC VISION:

Find a piece of art or a photograph and identify five different shapes you see. Next, focus on four lines or patterns, notice three colors, imagine two textures, and think of one emotion the artwork evokes.

SENSORY DISCOVERY:

Close your eyes and identify five different textures by touch. Then, listen for four unique sounds, take three deep breaths, name two things you can smell, and picture one serene place in your mind.

CLOUD COUNTING:

Look up at the sky and count five fluffy clouds, then four birds flying by, three leaves rustling in the wind, two passing (squirrels, creatures or cars) and one distant sound.

FLOWER WHISPERER:

Find a flower and observe its petals. Name five colors you see. listen for four soft sounds of nature. feel three different textures on the flower. notice two scents. and gently touch the petals as you count one deep breath.

<u>BODY SCAN</u>:

Close your eyes and feel five areas of your body that are in contact with a surface. Move on to notice four points of tension, three relaxed areas, two body sensations you hadn't noticed before, and one deep breath.

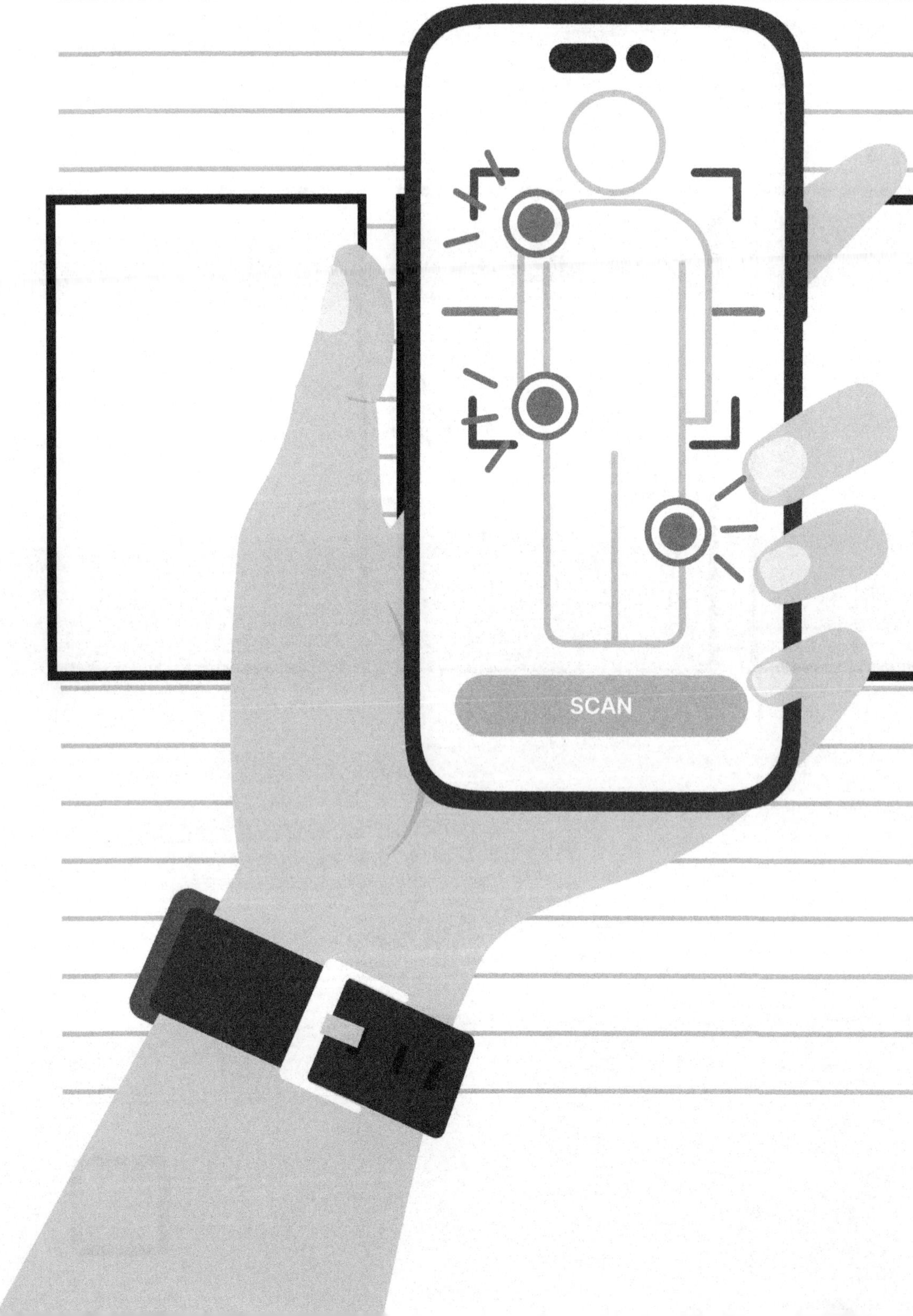

THE MIRACLE DAY:

If you were to wake up on a miraculous day, what differences would you notice at every step from morning until nightfall? Describe the day's activities and the changes that make it extraordinary, leading to a miraculous night. What would your friend observe as something different about you?

08.00

09.00

10.00

11.00

12.00

13.00

14.00

15.00

16.00

17.00

18.00

19.00

CHALLENGE EXCUSES:

Acknowledge and challenge excuses that hold you back. replacing them with action-oriented thoughts. Challenge them every day if you have do.

Monday	Tuesday
Wednesday	Thursday
Friday	Saturday
Sunday	Note

RED

Emotion: Red is often associated with intense emotions like love, passion, and anger. It can convey warmth, excitement, and energy. Imagine red as the color of a blazing dragon's breath, full of fiery passion and strong feelings like love and anger. It's like a thrilling rollercoaster ride for your emotions.

Psychological Effects: Red increases heart rate and stimulates appetite. It's known to grab attention and create a sense of urgency. In marketing, it's often used to draw focus and create a strong impression.

RED - "EMOTIONALLY CHARGED BREATHING"

- Close your eyes and take a deep breath in. As you exhale, imagine releasing any intense emotions like anger or frustration. Visualize the breath as a calming, cool breeze that soothes the fiery emotions. Repeat until you feel more centered.

ORANGE

Emotion: Orange is linked to feelings of creativity, enthusiasm, and warmth. It's an emotionally stimulating color. Think of orange as the color of a magical elixir that bubbles with creativity and enthusiasm, making you feel as if you're on an exciting adventure.

Psychological Effects: Orange is energizing and uplifting. It can promote a sense of fun and playfulness. It's often used in designs to add a touch of vitality.

ORANGE - "CREATIVE MINDFULNESS"

- Engage in a creative activity like drawing or painting with orange hues. Let the process be a form of mindfulness, where you focus on the strokes and colors. Allow your mind to wander and explore your creative side, embracing enthusiasm and playfulness.

YELLOW

EMOTION:

Yellow is associated with joy, happiness, and optimism. It radiates positivity. Picture yellow as the color of sunshine, spreading happiness and optimism wherever it goes. It's like a big, warm hug from your favorite book character.

PSYCHOLOGICAL EFFECTS:

Yellow stimulates mental activity and communication. It's known to be attention-grabbing and cheerful. In design, it's often used to evoke a sense of happiness and warmth.

YELLOW - "JOYFUL VISUALIZATION"

- Find a comfortable space and close your eyes. Imagine yourself in a serene, sunlit garden. Picture the vibrant yellow flowers and the warmth of the sun. Let this visualization fill you with joy and optimism, uplifting your spirits.

GREEN

EMOTION:
Green represents growth, balance, and harmony. It's often linked to nature and tranquility. Visualize green as the soothing shade of a secret forest grove, where you can find balance and harmony. It's your personal oasis of calm.

PSYCHOLOGICAL EFFECTS:
Green is calming and relaxing. It promotes a sense of peace and balance. It's used in design to create a soothing atmosphere.

GREEN - "NATURE'S TRANQUILITY"

- Spend time in a natural setting, like a park or garden. Sit quietly and observe the greenery around you. Pay attention to the rustling leaves and the harmony of nature. Let the calming green surroundings bring balance and inner peace.

BLUE

EMOTION:

Blue conveys calmness, trust, and serenity. It's often associated with feelings of stability and reliability. Imagine blue as the color of the calmest ocean you've ever seen, bringing feelings of trust and serenity. It's like a gentle lullaby for your soul.

PSYCHOLOGICAL EFFECTS:

Blue has a calming effect and can lower heart rate and blood pressure. It's used to create a sense of trustworthiness and professionalism in design.

BLUE - "BLUE SKY BREATHING"

- Step outside on a clear day and look up at the blue sky. Take a few deep breaths, inhaling the fresh air. As you exhale, imagine releasing any stress or tension, allowing it to float away like clouds in the vast blue sky. Repeat until you feel calm and serene.

INDIGO

EMOTION:

Indigo is linked to intuition, spirituality, and wisdom. It represents deep thought and introspection. Think of indigo as the mysterious night sky, where you can explore your deepest thoughts and tap into your inner wisdom. It's like a treasure hunt for your imagination.

PSYCHOLOGICAL EFFECTS:

Indigo encourages deep thinking and introspection. It's often associated with spirituality and meditation practices.

INDIGO - "INTROSPECTIVE JOURNALING"

- Set aside time for journaling in a quiet space. Write down your thoughts, questions, and reflections on life. Use indigo-colored ink or paper if possible. This deep introspection helps you connect with your inner wisdom and spirituality.

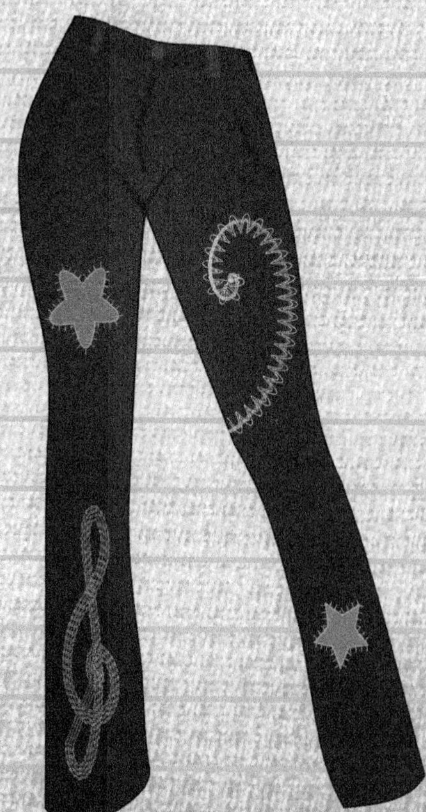

VIOLET

EMOTION:

Violet is connected to creativity, spirituality, and luxury. It's often seen as a mysterious and imaginative color. Picture violet as the color of a majestic castle, filled with creativity and luxury. It's where your wildest dreams and fanciest ideas come to life.

PSYCHOLOGICAL EFFECTS:

Violet is known to stimulate creativity and inspiration. It's used to convey a sense of luxury and elegance in design.

VIOLET - "CREATIVE DREAMSCAPE"

- Before bedtime, engage in creative writing or storytelling. Let your imagination run wild and create a whimsical or fantastical world. Incorporate violet elements into your story, such as purple landscapes or characters. This imaginative exercise fosters creativity and a sense of luxury.

REFLECT & CELEBRATE:

Regularly reflect on your progress, celebrating each small victory of your journey.

Printed in Great Britain
by Amazon

31073431R00079